Australia's Real
BAPTISM OF FIRE

Heroes known only to a few

Greg Raffin

First published by.
Five Senses Education Pty Ltd, 2013.
ABN 16 001 414 437
2/195 Prospect Highway,
Seven Hills NSW 2147

Printed by Five Senses Education Pty Ltd.

Cover image: AWM H19498

Raffin, Greg
'Australia's Real Baptism of Fire'
ISBN 978-1-74130-594-4

CONTENTS

FOREWORD

Early in Greg Raffin's marvellous book, "Australia's Real Baptism of Fire", he notes that while the veterans of 1914–1918 have all gone, interest in and commemoration of the events of that extraordinary period in Australia's history remains at a very high level — and in my view is at a greater pitch now than at any time in my life to date. I have the honour at the moment to be the Chairman of the New South Wales Advisory Council on the Centenary of Anzac. When Greg Raffin got in touch to mention his project to chronicle this hugely-interesting but mostly overlooked initial episode of Australia's war in 1914–18, I was both intrigued and delighted. Intrigued, because as a retired military man, I realised that while it was so significant to Australians then and now, very few people today knew anything about it; delighted, because even though the Australian Naval and Military Expeditionary Force heading off to New Guinea was a national effort, it sallied forth from Sydney in August 1914 very much led by the new Royal Australian Navy. In that regard, I want to recommend to you all that Greg Raffin's book is a major contribution to our knowledge beyond the historical norm, beyond Australia's involvement at Gallipoli, the Western Front and the Middle East. I hope we can appropriately commemorate the moment described in the book, in 2014.

If you are an avid consumer of military histories, you can be a bit apprehensive when you pick up a new work: is it going to be as dry as dust, forensically accurate but stupefyingly dull? Alternatively, will it be populist and haphazard without a 'spine' of historical rigour? Greg has walked the tight rope between two ends of the spectrum with consummate skill. He covers the preparations for and the deployments of the campaign, the landings, the fighting, the capitulation and the follow-up operations in a comprehensive and attractive way with frequent side-bar excursions to make his characters come alive. The handful of men killed during the fighting become known to us for their past and this makes the absence of their future beyond the 11th of September 1914 more poignant. Others as time goes by succumb to disease and accidents. Some are venal and some are criminal. All round out the story.

As important as was the military operation to seize German New Guinea, Greg Raffin's account of the first weeks and months and years of wartime colonial administration by Australia is a fascinating insight into an unexpected burden for a brand-new nation, Australia. While Greg informs us that Britain sought to retain rights over the ex-German colony, in all practical ways the greater New Guinea lands thus seized devolved to Australia at that time. It is interesting to theorise on the importance of our subsequent lengthy period of administrative control in contributing to Australia's grave concern in 1942 about the encroachment of Japan into New Guinea and the other parts of Germany's pre-World War I Pacific territories.

It is axiomatic that with so much written about the vast canvas which is Australia's involvement in the Great War, abundant remembrance and commemoration will be paid across the Centenary period to events in far off places. That is as it should be. Equally though there are other World War I stories which ought to be told and thus we all should be very grateful to Greg Raffin for his excellent work, a timely and eloquently written reminder of our men who were first to fight in August and September 1914.

Peter Cosgrove
General (Retd)

PREFACE

It was a miniscule blip on the radar of Time. Hostilities were basically over in one day. Current school History textbooks don't even mention it. A generation ago such textbooks gave, at best, a paragraph on it before going on to a detailed account of the Gallipoli campaign.

But the truth is that seven men died that September day in 1914. The occasion was the Australian takeover of German colonial possessions in New Guinea, just five weeks after the start of World War I.

This was truly Australia's "Baptism of Fire" even if it was only a quick immersion in the arena of battle. True, Australians had fought in the Boer War. They had even fought in Australian-based (as opposed to colonial) contingents. But this time those contingents were formed prior to, not during the hostilities.

The successful Australian takeover of German possessions in New Guinea and its surrounds ushered in a substantial and impressive list of "firsts" for this brash young nation. Yet there are few authoritative accounts on this campaign. Many of these are not readily available.

A number of the major nations of the world had acquired nationhood following lead-up conflicts. Germany was one such nation. Not so Australia. This nation, formulated without any military conflict would go on to prove itself quite competent in that arena… considering its youth. As is often the case with the young, there were mistakes. There were rogues. There were transgressions. And this was the same in the other battle arenas of World War I.

What will history say about this particular event? What is it about this event that piqued my interest in the New Guinea campaign of the First World War?

I was one of those pupils who read the brief references to German New Guinea and the sinking of the "Emden" before going on to learn about Gallipoli. I wanted to learn more; those who died in New Guinea deserved better.

When visiting the war cemeteries of the Western Front and Gallipoli both my wife and I were saddened by the graves marked *Known only to God*. This reminded me that there were Australians who had died and were buried in New Guinea during World War I "known only to a few".

I decided to do something about that.

Australia learnt a lot about military and naval strategies as a result of its experiences in New Guinea in 1914. But it also learnt a lot more than that. I have tried to reveal what was learnt by briefly referring to the period of administration which followed the initial hostilities.

During 2012 when I first set out to learn more about this campaign I thought I was re-telling a seldom-told story but as I did more research, I came to realise that it had far-reaching consequences. Consequences which went well beyond the time when it occurred. This realisation grew and, in my concluding chapters I have tried to put a case for viewing, with the benefit of hindsight, Australia's First World War New Guinea campaign in a different light.

I have added some "human interest" stories in my account of this historical event by weaving into it the personal backgrounds of three individuals all of whom had a role to play. Two of these men, Brian Pockley and Charles Elwell, were involved in the actual hostilities in

New Guinea; the other, William Miller, was a crew member on HMAS *Encounter* which stood guard near-by. William Miller's story is an unusual one; he served during World War 1 both as a member of the Royal Australian Navy and as a member of the Australian Imperial Forces. He was also my wife's Grandfather.

As the story progresses references to them diminishes. It is then that the stories of others, some of them key players, begin to emerge. I have also tried to briefly outline how the fates dealt with these men after the New Guinea campaign.

These stories are at times sad. At other times they are inspiring.

Despite the passage of almost a hundred years since that day of bravado in September, 1914 they are stories worth re-telling. Age shall not weary them.

Greg Raffin
July, 2013

ACKNOWLEDGEMENTS

Over twelve months ago I set out to learn more about the six men who died whilst helping Australia claim German's colonial possessions in New Guinea. As research into this area snowballed into the writing of this book I came into contact with a wide array of people who helped me in a variety of ways.

Early encouragement and advice came my way from Mr Ray Cooper, President of the Wauchope and District Historical Society. I am very grateful for his comments on my script. Nothing ever seemed to be a problem for Ray and help was always provided. Ray also worked on enhancing some of the photographs and maps.

I was also able to enlist the support and assistance of a former classmate who had far greater experience with publishing than I do. Mrs Jenny Eather was able to advise me on copyright issues, to review my script and to suggest appropriate adjustments. Her insights were always helpful and her suggested adjustments very precise.

Thank you both.

I was very honoured that General Peter Cosgrove agreed to write a Foreword for my book. As Chairman of the NSW Centenary of ANZAC Committee he has a key role in the commemoration of the centenary of the outbreak of World War I. He made suggestions regarding the launching of the book. I am very fortunate that he has lent his support and taken time from his busy schedule to do so.

As my research and writing progressed I was continually and pleasantly surprised by the number of people who willingly assisted me.

I am most appreciative of the support and assistance I received when researching material for this book. In particular I acknowledge the help I received from Mr Andrew Currey even though he was on leave from his normal role as a researcher at the Australian War Memorial. Mr Bill Edwards from the National Archives in Canberra provided a wealth of useful information. He was always most helpful.

I was pleased to be able to make contact with Tim and Simon Pockley, descendants of Captain Pockley's father, who were able to point me in the right direction and assist me in a number of ways. Mrs Toni Mundey, archivist at HMAS *Cerebus* provided important naval details. Ms Jenny Pearce, archivist at The Kings School, gave me relevant background details on and pictures of former pupils, Charles Elwell and Charles and Guy Manning.

I similarly acknowledge the advice provided by Mr John Perryman of the RAN Sea Power Centre. Mr John Smith, Senior Research Officer for the Naval Historical Society was kind enough to review two chapters which focused on Naval history and to point out necessary adjustments. Mr Russell King of Wauchope also reviewed some of my script and assisted me with the appendix.

I am fortunate in that I have been able to include a large number of relevant pictures to highlight the written word. I am deeply indebted to the Australian War Memorial for providing me with many of these pictures. I particularly acknowledge the assistance of Dr Brendan Nelson and Mr Mark Small. I also acknowledge the help of staff members Mr Ricky Phillips, Mr Craig Tebbitts and Ms Kelda McManus.

I was quite amazed at just how supportive people can be with a project such as this one. Whenever I approached people for copyright approval I received a positive outcome. I have endeavoured to acknowledge this fact in the appropriate manner through the references at the back of this book.

Then there came the matter of going into print. A friend, Pat O'Connor, was able to put me in touch with people in the printing business who he thought would help me. As a result I met Roger Furniss of "Five Senses Education". From the outset, Roger was interested in the material I had put together. He and his staff, Stuart Matthew and Naomi Kelly in particular, have been very supportive.

Without their assistance this book would not be in your hands.

Finally I would like to thank my wife Dot who listened patiently to my constant conversations about the events of this book and the process of putting it together.

Greg Raffin
July, 2013

TIMELINE OF EVENTS

1914

4 August	Great Britain declares war on Germany.
11 August	Enlistment for AN&MEF begins.
12 August	HMAS *Sydney* and destroyers raid Blanche Bay.
19 August	AN&MEF leave Sydney.
9 September	HMAS *Sydney* puts Nauru wireless station out of action.
11 September	AN&MEF lands on New Britain.
13 September	British flag hoisted at Rabaul.
17 September	Terms of Capitulation signed.
21 September	German and native troops lay down their arms.
24 September	AN&MEF occupy Madang.
17 October	AN&MEF occupies New Ireland.
6 November	AN&MEF occupy Nauru.
19 November	AN&MEF occupy Admiralty and Western Islands.
28 November	Tropical Force leaves Sydney.
9 December	AN&MEF occupy German Solomon Islands.

1915

8 January	Colonel Pethybridge takes over from Colonel Holmes.
9 January	AN&MEF begin to leave New Guinea; relieved by Tropical Force.

1921

9 May	End of Military Occupation of German New Guinea.

The footnotes (at the bottom of each page) relevant to personnel show their military ranks as at the end of WW I or their military career.

Chapter 1

GENESIS

"Fate rules the affairs of Mankind with no recognisable order."

(Seneca)

This is a story of a few brave men. It is also a story of a brash young nation. It is a story of an event which, like a beautiful flower, sprang quickly to life gaining great acclamation and yet just as quickly passed from the eye of the beholder.

The seeds of this story were sown in the eighth decade of the nineteenth century. Its culmination came in the second decade of the twentieth century, bringing together men from a diversity of backgrounds. The culmination also brought together a number of nations in a manner never before witnessed. The world was destined to be changed forever...

The destiny of the world was far from the minds of George and Annie Miller one cool but sunny October morning in 1886. After what can only be seen as a difficult birth under trying circumstances, the couple welcomed into the world their second child and first son, William. William's sister, Elizabeth had been born the previous year. Now their father had an even greater reason to ensure that he continued to work as a rural labourer on the grazing properties of the New England region near Armidale, New South Wales.

George Miller was a resourceful man and a good provider. He was ready to take on any kind of work in order to keep food on the table. Usually he worked on the nearby runs as a farm worker but occasionally he joined a team of shearers, usually in the role of a cook. He had met his wife-to-be during one of his brief breaks between shearing jobs. Annie was in her late teenage years and when she wasn't helping her mother with running their small home she sometimes worked as a cook. Friends said they made a loving couple and no one was surprised when George decided to ask Annie to marry him.

Annie became a devoted wife and was soon the proud mother of Elizabeth. She had no difficulties with her first pregnancy but the cold New England winter took a toll on her health and so her second pregnancy was not an easy one for her. To add to her problems the baby came early and the midwife was late in arriving to assist. William was a small baby but in his favour was the fact that the days were slowly starting to warm as summer approached.

George and Annie lived in a small hut on the western outskirts of Armidale which George had begun to build soon after he met Annie. As time went by William grew in strength and size. Good seasons meant there was plenty of work for George and so their family also grew in size. Gilah was born in 1888 and a second son, George junior was born in 1890. Annie was assisted from time to time by her mother who lived nearby, closer to the centre of town.

William, his two sisters and brother were able to form a strong affinity with the bush. As they grew up they would spend hours exploring nearby bushland whenever they could escape from the never-ending chores or the need to attend to their schooling. Often their chores involved looking after their younger siblings. George and Annie added a further three girls and two boys to their family as the nineties progressed and the new century arrived. The children were brought up in a rough and ready manner in a loving household with firm but fair parents…

A world away and a few years earlier than the birth of William, another family had witnessed the arrival of a son. In the village of Albrighton on the eastern edge of Shropshire, England and on a cool September morning in 1882 a proud Elwell senior welcomed a son who was later christened Charles Bingham Elwell. The Elwell family enjoyed a more affluent lifestyle than that of the Miller family. Elwell senior was also better educated as he possessed skills which were later to make him suitable as a migrant to the distant colony of New South Wales. His full name was Paul Bedford Elwell and he had wed Elizabeth Jane Louise Thorn in 1879 in Middlesex County. Her father, William, had been an attorney when he wed Anna, who was born in County Kildare, Ireland.

Charles Elwell was born at a time when the days were growing shorter and a severe English winter approached. Charles did have the opportunity to gain a better and broader education than William Miller. The countryside which he explored was the undulating hills of Shropshire; it was greatly different to the heavily timbered and steep slopes of the New England area. His days were spent, not so often in the company of his parents but with teachers who were to skill him in a number of ways, including the ability to speak fluent French. He further developed this gift by travelling to France from time to time.

Unlike William Miller who usually walked barefoot to the small local school in Armidale, Charles wore stout leather boots to protect his feet from the cold.

Charles developed a certain precision and attention to detail from his father. He was destined to develop as a man who, when he did things, he did them well. Family life taught him respect for his elders and a sense of his true place in the order of things. Charles developed a strong sense of history and the role played by fate on the outcome of personal events. There were four children in the Elwell family. Charles had just one sister, Essie Violet and two brothers, Paul Leonard and Lawrence Bedford Elwell. Only one of the nine Miller children, James Robert Miller, had been given a second Christian name…

Four years after the birth of William Miller, a well-appointed home in the leafy Sydney suburb of Wahroonga celebrated the arrival of a second son and the third of five children. Brian Colden Antill Pockley was born at St. Leonards on 4th June 1890 to Helen and Dr. Francis Antill Pockley. Brian Pockley became part of a well-known and well-repected family. His family background was a great influence on the path he was to take in life.

Dr. Francis Antill Pockley was a Macquarie Street (Sydney) eye specialist and was also at one time, the President of the NSW Branch of the British Medical Association. Francis' father was Captain Robert Francis Pockley. In 1885 he married Helen, the grand-daughter of Captain Henry Colden Antill, aide-de-camp to Governor Lachlan Macquarie. Thus both Francis and Helen Pockley had ancestors with a military background. Born in the midst of a coastal winter, Brian Pockley came from both a medical and a military background.

The Pockley family consisted of five children. Phyllis Antill Pockley was born in 1886, Francis in 1888; John Graham Pockley and Helen Dorothy Pockley were born after Brian, in 1891 and 1895 respectively. Their childhood had much more in common with Charles Bingham than it did with William Miller. Formal education was much more structured, involving private schools and they were given every opportunity to develop their education. Neither the Elwell parents in Shropshire nor the Pockley parents in Sydney had to spend as much time ensuring that they had regular employment and a steady supply of food for their family as did George Miller in Armidale. Social outings also were much more structured than the spontaneous ramblings in the bush in which the Miller children took part. The Pockley children would go on picnics and boat trips with friends and cousins. William Miller and his brother George, would at times escape to the bush at short notice and with little planning beforehand…

As the seasons progressed and the children grew, developments occurred in the world about them. Throughout their different, but happy childhoods, storm clouds began to develop in places removed from where they were growing up. At first these clouds only involved people in high places; people with political power and influence. So engrossed were most people with their daily concerns they did not really know, nor care about the storms building up about them. Yet the changes occurring were beginning to emerge at a quickening pace. Soon they would become impossible to ignore. Later they would also be impossible to avoid.

These changes were to enmesh all of the powerful nations of the world. They were to change the destiny of the world. They were also to have an impact on the destinies of William Miller, Charles Bingham and Brian Pockley. Unbeknown to them they were destined to be brought together in a manner and in a place about which they knew very little.

Chapter 2

THE RACE FOR EMPIRE

The truth is that...Imperialism...has always been driven by strategic interests.

(Charley Reese)

The seeds of World War 1 were sown well before its outbreak in 1914. As a result of its defeat in the Franco-Prussian War (1871) France was imbued with a desire for "revanche" (revenge).

The French defeat was costly for that nation. It lost significant territory (e.g. Alsace-Lorraine) and was forced to pay reparations. But worst of all was the loss of prestige. The status of France as a leading world power was seriously dented.

French politicians set about forming a series of (usually secretive) political and military alliances that were designed to isolate her arch-enemy, Germany. They were determined to ensure that the neighbouring power never again achieved a position of dominance.

These political-military developments of the late nineteenth century were not the only significant developments. Economic developments, ushered in gently at first, by the Agrarian and Industrial revolutions were coming to a head. For a variety of reasons Great Britain was the leading industrial power but its hegemony was being challenged by Germany, France and across the Atlantic, the United States.

Development as an industrial power was dependent on a number of foundation stones. Two of the more important were access to raw materials and the availability of markets for the finished product. So, for example, Britain gained wool from the Australian colonies; it sold some of its textile goods to the Indian colonies.

The would-be industrial power which also had an overseas empire had a distinct economic advantage. But colonial possessions could also be acquired for purposes of military strategy. Gibraltar, for example, at the entrance to the Mediterranean Sea was valued by the British. But some colonies in reality had little economic or strategic value. They had been acquired to enhance national prestige. Some of the possessions of various European powers on the continent of Africa did not have major economic or strategic value…

The economic changes taking place in Europe also had an impact on those living in European colonies across the world. The 1880s had been a period of prosperity for the Australia colonies and George Miller had seldom been out of work. His family had grown in size and so too had the children of he and Annie. They had provided the beginnings of a basic education for William and his siblings at the local small school on the western fringes of Armidale. He had attended school regularly other than when he was required to help out at home. At school he was part of a large class of students carrying slates and firmly under the control of a stern master who had received his training under the teacher-mentor system supervised by an experienced colleague. William's education was centred on the three R's; reading, 'riting and 'rithmetic; there was also nature study and some history but no foreign languages.

The 1880s were becoming a period of prosperity and central to this prosperity was the continued growth of railway networks throughout the colony which had begun in the 1860s. This had been accompanied by prosperity in rural areas, now that it was easier to get products like wool to market but also due to a succession of favourable seasons. The early "squatters" of the New England region were now becoming wealthy pastoralists.

Then, as now, "boom" is often followed by "bust". As the 1890s arrived so too did a succession of droughts. The impact of these on people working in the pastoral industry was catastrophic. George Miller soon found it increasingly difficult to get work as a shearer's cook. He supplemented his income working at odd jobs wherever and whenever he could get them. As this decade progressed he saw value in trying to get permanent work on the railways. When he was finally able to do this it eased the pressure on his family, but it also meant that he later had to move most of his family to Sydney in order to retain his job…

Railways were also significant in the destiny of the Bingham family in England. For a variety of reasons Paul Elwell decided to move his family in order to secure their future. When Charles Elwell was about eight years of age the family made the decision to migrate to New South Wales, the first of the British colonies on the "Great South Land", soon to become the nation of Australia. They moved to Wentworthville, an area to the north-west of Sydney and Paul Elwell began work with Railways in NSW. He became their Chief Electrical Engineer.

Wentworthville was some distance from the centre of Sydney and so young Charles Elwell now had the opportunity to explore the Australian bush in a way similar to the excursions of William Miller in Armidale. However his education continued to be structured and to offer a variety of subjects beyond the basic three R's. From 1892 to 1896 he attended the nearby King's School at Parramatta. One of the few day boys there, he was in the company of children from wealthy and privileged backgrounds. Day boys were not allowed to wear the school uniform but they did receive tuition in a wide array of subjects. For example, Charles was able to study French. The King's School developed a proud history and remains today as one of Australia's most prestigious schools. A fellow school pupil was Charles Edye Manning. These men were destined to meet again in a different place and under different circumstances…

During this same period Brian Pockley furthured his education was also furthered by attending a prestigious Sydney private school. His father, Francis, enrolled Brian at the exclusive Shore school on the lower north shore of Sydney Harbour, across from the city of Sydney and not too far from his father's medical practice in Macquarie Street. He too was offered an education in not only the basic subjects but also a variety of other subjects and activities.

Brian was to prove a model student in a wide array of pursuits:

"He was a champion athlete of the school and won the championship shield two years running, with a record number of points on each occasion. He also captained the college football team for two years and during that time the team was unbeaten. He gained two scholarships while at the college." (1)

Brian Pockley maintained the family's military connection. He became a member of the school's cadets, soon showing he was as a crack shot. In other ways his life altered little. The economic security of the family was assured; the family outings and picnics continued. Brian was a popular figure at the school. He was well-liked by both his school mates and close members of his family. More significantly he developed as a caring person; this trait was to serve him well in his chosen career. Both he and his father were keen for him to enter the medical profession...

Meanwhile as the nineteenth century drew to a close, a significant build-up of distrust and rivalry was brewing around the world, particularly in Europe...

In no other sphere was this more evident than the "Race for Empire". Each power wanted to outdo its rival, to enhance its own status. Acquisition of overseas colonies frequently became a means to that end. Rivalry over colonial possessions in Africa inflamed an intense situation. Rivalry, nationalism and racial tensions ensured that the Balkans area became "the powder keg of Europe". By comparison, events involving New Guinea, the world's second largest island, were a sideshow. However interest in this area had been developing over many years...

Early European interest in New Guinea

New Guinea first came to European and world attention as the result of colonial rivalry between Portugal and Spain during the fifteenth century. Their real interest was in the lucrative Spice Islands and New Guinea was passed when travelling to or from the Americas. The north coast of this island was discovered by the end of the sixteenth century and in 1606 de Torres of Spain passed through the strait which now bears his name.

Later in that same year a Dutchman, Willem Jansz, sailed along the west and south coasts of New Guinea. Like de Torres, Jansz took little interest in the area other than naming key geographical features on the coastline. The same can be said about the interest shown by William Dampier, the English buccaneer and explorer. He apparently was as underwhelmed about the area and its people as he was by the north-west coast of Australia. He had referred to the inhabitants there as the "miserablest people on the earth". It was also he who named the large island, "New Britain".

Some sixty-seven years later (1766-7) another Englishman, Carteret, was sent on a specific voyage of exploration. He found a separate island near to New Britain which he called "New Ireland" and the intervening channel he called "St George's Channel".

Cartaret actually took possession of the country, with all the neighbouring islands, for the King of Great Britain. He nailed a lead-lined board to a tall tree. On it he engraved the date and time, his name and that of his vessel plus a drawing of the Union flag of England. No remnant of this plaque remains today.

Two figures, significant to Australia also passed by the area. These were James Cook (1770) and William Bligh (1792). Cook and Bligh had little interest in the area as they were merely islands enroute to other destinations.

It was also about this time that an interest in trade with this area was shown for the first time. In 1793 the British East India Company sent two ships to New Guinea to investigate the possibility of trade. On 10 July 1793 Captain Bampton (of the *Cornwallis*) again hoisted the

British flag (on Darnley Island) taking possession of New Guinea and the neighbouring islands.

However no long-term trade contact was established despite the fact that British troops did occupy what was then known as Manaswari Island in Geelvink Bay for a few months. Conditions were severe for the troops; their relief following their departure was significant.

Throughout the 1700s, and particularly the 1800s, a number of French and British exploratory excursions took place. These included voyages by Bougainville (1769) and D'Entrecasteaux (1793), the latter searching for the lost French explorer, La Perouse.

In 1846 Lieutenant Yule, in the *Bramble* again took formal possession of the New Guinea coastline on behalf of the British Crown. This was at a time when Britain was opening new colonies in the Pacific region, particularly on the Australian mainland.

Thus by 1880 British explorers had done the main work of surveying and tracing the New Guinea coastline. They had also shown an interest in commerce in the area. The British had formally annexed various islands and parts of New Guinea on behalf of Great Britain on three occasions: Carteret (1767), Bampton (1793) and Yule (1846).

By comparison, only one German explorer, Finsch, had done any real exploration in the area. Between 1875 and 1887 he made five exploratory voyages along part of the New Guinea coast. Germany was the last European nation to contribute to the exploration of this area. It entered this field of endeavour only after the basic pioneering exploratory work had been done by other nations.

Colonial concerns and German subterfuge

In the 1880s there was no Australian national government, only separate colonial governments. However there was a growing sense of nationalism – a desire to be seen as, and to act, as one.

Some of this sentiment was racist. For several decades there had been a strong desire to exclude Asians, particularly the Chinese, from coming to Australia. There was also concern over the economic and social impact of the importation of Kanaka workers into Queensland. Coupled with this was the realisation that such problems could only be dealt with by putting on a united front. Back in the heady goldrush days of the mid-nineteenth century the colony of Victoria had tried to stop ships berthing at Melbourne from off-loading any Asiatic passengers. They passed legislation to achieve this only to find the ship would continue onto Adelaide from where the unwanted orientals would simply walk overland to the goldfields.

As communications technology developed the size of the globe shrank. Improvements in communications meant that news from Europe could (by the second half of the nineteenth century) reach Australia much more quickly than before. Stuart's successful journey across the continent from south to north had been quickly followed (in 1872) by the building of the telegraph line, which was widely regarded as a significant engineering achievement. Meanwhile the power of the leading European nations grew.

So it was that concerns in Australia led to such developments as the construction of an armed fortress (Fort Dennison) in Sydney Harbor. This came as the result of a perceived potential threat from Russia during the Crimean War.

It was from this background that New South Wales, in co-operation with its Queensland counterparts urged the British government to take formal possession of the north-east coast of New Guinea. Heartfelt appeals were made in 1864, 1874, 1878 and again in 1879 but each time these fell on deaf ears. Matters came to a head when on 4th April, 1883, Chester, the resident magistrate at Thursday Island acting under direction from the Queensland government took possession of all of the non-Dutch part of New Guinea and the adjacent islands.

This action was not supported by the British government. Basically the British "washed their hands of the whole affair". In their defence it must be said that they faced other, more pressing concerns as significant problems had arisen in Egypt and in other parts of Africa. Britain was developing its relationship with the French who were in turn fearful of Germany.

Another key factor was the tactic of subterfuge employed by Germany. German diplomats repeatedly assured the British that they had no intentions of laying claim to the British archipelago. Britain in turn tried to explain to those in Australia that a declaration of sovereignty by Great Britain over New Guinea would be an unfriendly act towards Germany, a nation friendly to Britain.

It would seem that the British were more prepared to dismay the distant colonials than they were to upset the nearby and powerful Germans. The ultimate decision over matters such as this was a British, not a colonial, decision. And dismay the colonials they did. The Victorian premier, James Service, informed the foreign office on Christmas Eve, 1884:

"The exasperation here is boundless. We protest in the name of the present and future of Australia. If England does not save us from the danger and disgrace, as far at least as New Guinea is concerned, the bitterness of feeling towards her will not die out with this generation." (2)

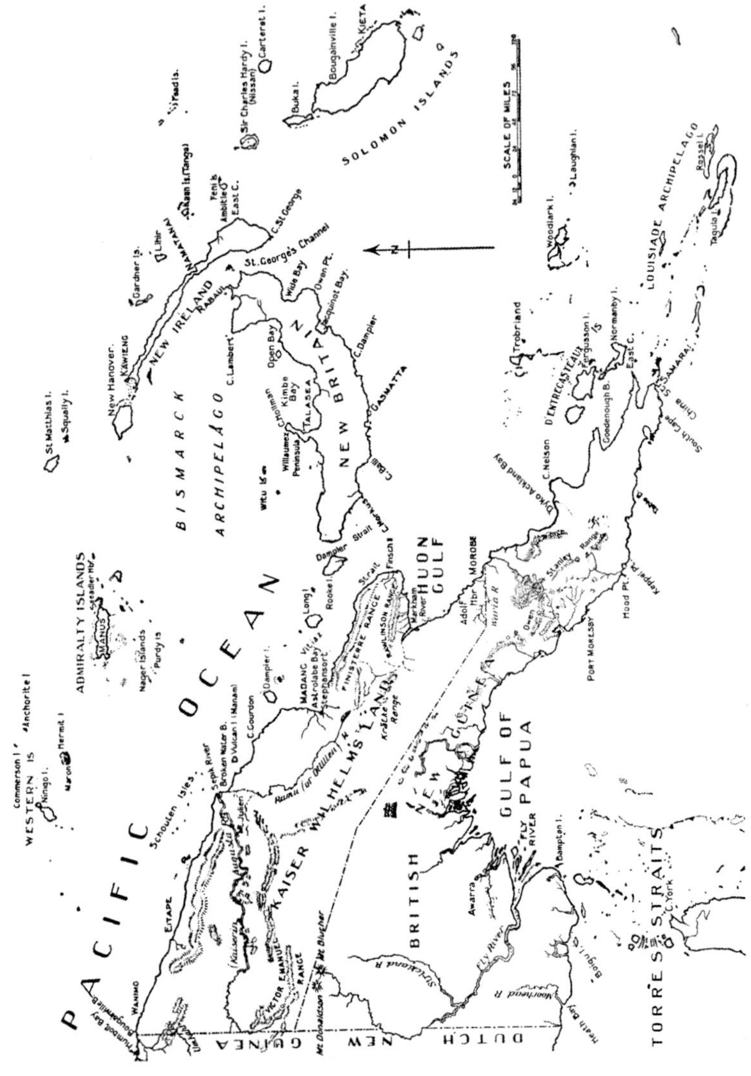

German New Guinea – 1914
(Official History of WWI - C.E.W. Bean)

Germany seizes the moment

Germany quickly took advantage of the British blunder. Throughout November 1884 it hoisted its flag in various locations in north-eastern New Guinea. It officially notified the British government of its actions on 19th December, 1884. Throughout 1885 several places were re-named. The New Britain Archipelago became "Bismarck Archipelago"; New Britain became "Neu Pommen" and the German portion of New Guinea was to be known as "Kaiser Wilhelm's Land". By 13th November 1886 Germany had also claimed control over the Solomon Islands.

German actions in New Guinea were not simply to enhance her prestige as a colonial power. Observers in Australia feared that Germany's intention was to build up her naval power in the Pacific region. That this was a key concern is borne out by subsequent German actions. Germany established a naval base at Tsingtao (China) in 1897. In 1899 she purchased the Marshall and Caroline Islands from Spain. Germany also acquired a strategic base from which an attack on New Zealand could be launched when she gained control over Samoa (1900).

Whilst strategic reasons were to the fore they were not the sole German motivation. Her new western Pacific possessions would give her a sound base from which to share in the trade and commerce of that region.

There was also a desire from within Germany for the new European power to be seen as a great colonial power as were Britain and France. Unlike the former, Germany did not have a lot of time to build up the influence of those colonies. The answer to this situation was to pour vast amounts of money into their new colonial areas. So it was that towns like Rabaul were transformed. Large German trading companies were given extensive encouragement and assistance to facilitate this process. The German government subsidised steamship services and encouraged tropical agriculture.

"By the year 1914 Germany was an important factor in the trade of the Pacific. And always behind this commercial expansion there was suspected a primary aim-to increase her naval power in the Pacific." (3)

As far as New Guinea was concerned the Germans did indeed build a significant naval presence. In fact the extent of their military build-up in this area was greater than many expected.

Key political figures in Australia were very concerned about these developments and in particular those related to increasing German involvement in the area. In the context of the growing tension between the nations of Europe it was only a matter of time before something would need to be done about the emerging situation.

Chapter 3

DUTY CALLS

"Australia will stand behind our Mother Country to help and defend her to our last man and our last shilling."

(Andrew Fisher, Australian Prime Minister)

Arguments about German activities in the south-west Pacific and discussions about political tensions in Europe were not the key concerns of those going about their daily lives in Australia. During the first decade of the twentieth century William Miller, Charles Elwell and Brian Pockley probably spent little time pondering the significance of events occurring on the other side of the world...

Just before the turn of the century George Miller senior, now working for the railways, moved his family to Elizabeth Street, Redfern, near to Sydney's new railway terminus. His wife, Annie, was able to gain work as a cook in a nearby restaurant which provided food for both city workers and weary travellers.

William and the younger members of the Miller family were still coming to terms with the need to develop at least a basic education. William was particularly keen to get some sort of employment but, being relatively small in stature, he found it difficult to get labouring work. On the other hand with his blue eyes, dark brown hair and easy-going manner he did get on well with people. He would often go off to work with his mother and help her in the kitchen whenever he could.

William would run errands, make the tea and throw out the scraps. He soon learnt the rudiments of wholesome cooking and also how the waiting staff should attend to customers of the restaurant. Although of humble background himself this gave him the opportunity to learn about the lifestyle and mannerisms of those who came from a more privileged background. At the same time he furthered his informal education. William proved to be a quick learner. This was to be of great benefit to him in coming years.

Subject as he was to the needs of those who paid him he was not subject to any military discipline. He still enjoyed his times with his younger brothers and sisters although he did miss the company of his brother, George, who had initially come to Sydney with the family, but later returned to search for work in the Armidale area.

There was one other setback for William during these early years. In 1908 he became quite ill and suffered serious abdominal pain. The family was not able to readily afford the services of a good doctor and so it was some time before he was diagnosed with acute appendicitis. By this time the severity of the pain had increased and so too had the need to deal with it quickly. He was quickly operated on and the appendix was removed. However, the operation was not well-performed and this was to become a recurrent problem for him…

Whilst there was little of a military nature in the life of William Miller in the early years of the twentieth century, the situation was vastly different for Charles Elwell.

Lieutenant Commander Charles Bingham Elwell
Courtesy The King's School, Parramatta

At the age of sixteen Charles Bingham Elwell joined the Royal Navy. He became a model officer and on 15th October 1898 was appointed a midshipman. Charles was very conscientious and also willing to learn. As a result promotion came rapidly. He was promoted to Sub-Lieutenant on 15 April 1902 and to Lieutenant on 30 June 1904. During these and the following years he was trained, tested and found competent in a variety of naval skills including Navigation, Pilotage, Gunnery and Torpedo training.

Spending some time in France he honed his knowledge of the French language and as a result he became fluent in French. He applied for the position of interpreter but his application was passed over. His superiors invariably reported that he was extremely zealous and attentive but lacking in experience as an executive officer. A certain Captain Chambers believed he showed great promise and took a great interest in all relevant matters.

As a result of his training and service he was promoted to Lieutenant-Commander on 30 June 1912. In Britain he served on such ships as *Britannia, Impregnable* and *Andromeda*. In 1913 he was seconded by the British to the new Navy of the Australian Commonwealth government and placed on board HMAS *Melbourne*. (1)

From the start of 1914 he was attached to the Royal Naval College at Geelong, Victoria, as a skilled instructor. As well as his competence he had great charm of manner and this meant he was extremely popular with the cadets at Geelong. Charles was quiet in speech but full of energy both in work and at games. In addition he coached the College's boat crew.

As an instructor Charles was well aware of the need to lead by example. His role as an officer in command of others also taught him to be concerned for their welfare. He was developing as a man well-suited to the role of leadership and it is in this role that History will remember him.

Later that year Charles Bingham Elwell was appointed to command the Royal Naval Reservists who went with the Australian Naval and Military Expeditionary Force (AN&MEF)...

During these early years of the twentieth century life for Brian Pockley continued in much the same manner as it had during his earlier school years. He had been one of the earliest pupils of St Andrew's Sunday school. As a result of a good home influence he had developed a moral and upright character.

He entered Sydney University to study medicine ultimately taking his M.B. and C. M. degrees. Sport continued to be an important part of his life. A member of the University's Rugby First fifteen, he was regarded as one of the best-ever three-quarters to play for them. Brian was Secretary of the University Athletic Club and also Secretary of the University Medical Society.As was the case when at school he continued to be popular; it was said that he was one of the most popular students at the University. (2)

When not at his studies Brian Pockley enjoyed a variety of social activities. April, 1912 he wrote to his aunty "Dear Old Nellikens" telling her of his recent camping trip to the Hawkesbury (a river on the northern outskirts of Sydney) and how they had enjoyed their time at the family's houseboat. They were fishing and camping for some time as he mildly complained about how sore his face was after scraping off a ten-day beard growth. However their initial inability to catch fish had passed and they were able to catch nineteen big flathead.

"I found 14 letters waiting for me when I got back and as I already had some I owed, I guess I will spend most of my time for a week or two writing letters as hard as I can go..."

As part of such trips Brian was developing his skills as a cook of plain but wholesome foods. He considered himself a "lovely cook" of "fried and boiled fish, porridge, fried bacon and eggs, boiled potato and onions"... (3)

Declaration of War

When Great Britain declared war on Germany (4th August, 1914) there was widespread support for the Mother Country from both the press and the public. Both of the two major political parties were in favour of lending assistance as soon as possible. Given that about 80% of the Australian population were either born in Great Britain or descended from people born in Great Britain, this was not surprising.

Within days of the declaration of war by Britain the Australian government had set about forming the Australian Imperial Forces and had promised to provide 20,000 men to aid Britain's needs. This number was more than doubled within a few days as men rushed to volunteer. By December 1914, 52,000 men had signed up to join the AIF.

Nor did the British waste any time in allocating to the fledgling Australian government a specific task for it to carry out. On 8th August it telegrammed a request:

"If your Ministers desire and feel themselves able to seize the German wireless stations at Yap in the Marshall Islands, Nauru (or) Pleasant Island and New Guinea, we should feel that this was a great and urgent Imperial service."(4)

The British were also at pains to point out that any territory occupied as a result of this request would be considered a British possession and therefore a British decision would decide the destiny of that area at the ultimate conclusion of the war. Their sense of Empire was greater than their sense of geography as Yap was actually part of the Caroline Islands.

Australia's response to the British suggestion/order was rapid. The new Chief of the General Staff, Colonel J.G. Legge[1] made the organisation of a force to achieve this task one of his primary aims. Given the fact that the objectives were some distance away from each other it was decided to form a combined naval and military force, "the Australian Naval and Military Expeditionary Force" (AN&MEF). In an effort to accomplish the task quickly the entire infantry section (a battalion of 1023 men) plus the machine gun and signalling sections and the medical complement were all to be enlisted from NSW. (5)

Six companies from the Royal Australian Naval reserve were gathered from NSW, Victoria, Queensland and South Australia. Companies 1, 2 and 3 came from NSW, Nos. 4 and 5 from Victoria whilst No. 6 company mainly consisted of men from South Australia. Some Queensland personnel were attached to the NSW companies. Each company consisted of about 50 men under the command of a Lieutenant. Provision was made for a further subdivision into left and right half companies each of which was led by a junior officer, usually a midshipman. (6).

A force of troops was also raised from New Zealand and these troops were accompanied by HMA Ships *Australia* and *Melbourne.* HM Ships *Psyche, Philomel, Pyramus* and the French cruiser *Montcalm*

1 Colonel Legge, (later Major-General), organised and commanded the 2nd Aust. Div. in Gallipoli and France.

landed on the Samoan island of Apia on 30th August, 1914 and German Samoa was surrendered without a fight. HMAS *"Australia"* was sent on to Nauru to destroy the German radio station there. *"Australia"* arrived on 9th September to find the radio station had already been disabled and Nauru also surrendered without opposition.

The major Australian task was the takeover of German New Guinea. The complete Australian naval force consisted of the *Australia, Sydney, Encounter, Melbourne, Warrego, Yarra, Parramatta,* the submarines *AE1* and *AE2*, the submarine tenders, *Protector* and *Upolu*, a supply ship the *Aorangi*, three colliers and the former P & O liner *Berrima*. (7)

Less than a year earlier (4th October 1913) the Australian fleet consisting of the battle cruiser *Australia*, light cruiser *Sydney*, cruisers *Melbourne* and *Encounter*, destroyers *Warrego, Parramatta* and *Yarra* had sailed into Sydney Harbor where they were enthusiastically welcomed by the people of Sydney.

German Military and Naval strength in the SW Pacific and New Guinea.

At the start of the war the German Naval strength in the region was impressive. Their flagship under Rear-Admiral von Spee was the cruiser *Scharnhorst*. It was accompanied by four other cruisers: *Gneisenau, Emden, Leipzig* and *Nurnberg* as well as the small cruisers *Cormoran* and *Geier*. The *Scharnhorst* and the *Gneisenau* were first-class armoured cruisers with 8.2 inch guns. Only one Australian vessel, the battle-cruiser *Australia*, had bigger guns but of those sent to New

Guinea the vessel with the biggest guns mounted was the *Encounter* which had eleven 6-inch guns. (8)

Within the area of the German Protectorate there was no standing army but there were personnel who had military training. A former cavalry captain was charged with the task of training and arming a native police force. The colonial budget provided funds for a force in the order of 1000 members.The only men with a military background belonged to the reserve and *Landwehr* of the German Army. Once all such personnel had reported for service the armed force comprised two officers on the active list of the German Army, seven *Landwehr* officers, 52 white non-commissioned officers and men and about 240 native soldiers. The two regular officers were Captain of Cavalry von Klewitz (placed in charge of the troops) and Senior Lieutenant Mayer who was placed in command of the native expeditionary force. (9)

Assuming all forces from both sides were assembled in the one place and at the same time it would seem that the AN&MEF had the advantage in terms of military numbers. It may have been that the Australians were at a serious disadvantage in terms of naval firepower. Their greatest advantage was the degree to which Germany was prepared to defend its radio bases given that she was entering a life or death struggle in Europe.

The Germans had no colonial defence force (Schutztruppe); the Polizeitruppe was formed to put down rebellions and intervene in tribal wars. This group had proved effective in putting down the Sokehs rebellion of 1910 and they had learnt from this experience. However half of the native members were untrained and many of the white soldiers were only partly trained reservists.

Colonel Holmes
AWM:A05789

Leadership of the Australian Naval and Military expeditionary force

The man chosen to lead the AN&MEF came from a family with a military background and had an impressive military background himself. William Holmes[2] was born in 1862, the son of former British Army Officer, Captain William Holmes. At that time he was chief clerk at headquarters of the NSW Military Forces. His mother, Jane, was the daughter of Patrick Hackett of the 11th Foot. Until his marriage in 1887, William lived at Victoria Barracks.

Holmes joined the 1st Infantry Regiment, NSW Military Forces at an early age; he was a bugler at age 10. He served at almost every rank rising to the rank of Major and assuming overall command in 1903. In 1899 he volunteered for active service in the Boer War with the NSW Infantry contingent and although a captain at the time he accepted a position as a lieutenant. Later he was promoted to Captain commanding 'E' squadron, 1st NSW Mounted Rifles. He saw action at Colesburg, Pretoria and Diamond Hill. He was awarded a Distinguished Service Order, mentioned in despatches and promoted to Brevet-Lieutenant-Colonel.

Apart from the period of his service in the Boer War his defence work was not his fulltime occupation. Before the Boer War he joined the Metropolitan Board of Water Supply and Sewerage, rising to the position of Secretary in 1895. He returned to that position after the war but maintained his voluntary military service. His civilian role further developed his capacity to organise and administer. It also gave him a greater knowledge of men.

2 Major-General W.Holmes, CMG, DSO, V.D.,Commanded AN&MEF 1914/15; 5th Inf. Bde. 1915/16; 4th Div., 1916/17; b. Sydney, 12 Sept. 1862. Killed in action, Flanders, 2 July, 1917.

From 1902 to 1911 Holmes was Lieutenant-Colonel commanding the 1st Australian Infantry Regiment and from August, 1912 he was Colonel of 6th Infantry Brigade. After the introduction of compulsory military training in 1910 he became involved in rifle-shooting competitions. He introduced the first fire and movement competitions in the Australian Army (under the title of The Governor's Cup) (10).

Holmes chose as his brigade-major, Major Heritage[3], Commandant of the Commonwealth School of Musketry at Randwick. This man had considerable experience and was also a man of tact. He was to show his true leadership abilities in the events following the assault on the German defences. To command the battalion of infantry he called upon Lieutenant-Colonel Russell Watson[4]. Watson had a genial personality, was able to relate well with his officers but at the same time could assert his authority when such was required. His expertise and skill in the area of training recruits later became apparent and led to subsequent appointments in that field.

The role of Principal Medical Officer went to Lieutenant-Colonel Howse[5] who had gained a high professional reputation for his role in the South African War. Howse had been awarded the Victoria Cross for gallant rescue work under heavy fire during that campaign.

Two appointments of passing interest were made. Captain Travers[6] of the Australian Intelligence Corps was made staff-captain

3 Brig. FB Heritage, C.B.E., M.V.O., Commanded Aust. Corps School 1917/18, Commandant Royal Military College of Australia,1922/29, 1931/32, Commandant 2nd Military District 1929/32, Q.M.G. 1933-34, b.Tasmania, 21 Sept.1877.

4 Col. WW Russell Watson, C.B., CMG,V.D., Commanded 24th Btn. 1915/17, Overseas Training Brigade 1917/19, Company Director of Balmain, b. Sydney 19 May, 1875.

5 Major-General Hon.Sir Neville R. Howse, VC, KCB, KCMG, DMS,AIF 1915/19, Minister for Defence 1925/27,Health 1925/27,1928/29, Home and Territories 1928, Repatriation 1928/29, of Orange, NSW, b. Somerset, England, 26 Oct. 1863.

6 Lt.-Col. RJA Travers, DSO, Commanded 26th Btn. AIF, 1916/18, Draughtsman of Bondi, b. Glen Innes, NSW, 21 April, 1888.

and intelligence officer. Travis was Holmes' son-in-law. Lieutenant Basil Holmes[7] was made Aide-de-camp for the expedition. He was William Holmes' son. (11)

This was not the only instance of a family connection amongst the leadership of the AN&MEF. Keith Heritage[8], the brother of Major Francis Bede Heritage, became the transport officer. Keith Heritage, who later went on to be awarded the Military Cross, was killed at Pozieres. He is credited with being the first man to volunteer for the newly-formed AIF (12)

Second-in-command of the regimental staff (under Lieutenant-Colonel Watson) was Major J. Paton[9]. Captain C.H.D. Lane of Bondi was appointed as adjutant. The role of Quartermaster went to Captain S.P. Goodsell. (13)

These men were designated as leaders. It is interesting that few of them had a military background but that didn't exclude them as men of great leadership potential. When following their subsequent careers it becomes apparent that many were directed into areas of expertise in which they displayed considerable skill during the New Guinea campaign.

Leadership and War were to leave their marks on each of them. For some the outcome would be disastrous; others would go on to renown. Neither they nor the major nations of the world would ever be the same again. Many men would fall but so too would Empires.

---

7 Lieut.-Col. B Holmes, DSO, 17th Btn. AIF, Orchardist of Sydney, b. 11 September, 1892.

8 Capt. K.Heritage, M.C. 19th Btn. Traffic Manager, b. Longford, Tas., Killed in France, 26 July 1916.

9 Maj.-Gen. J. Paton, C.B., CMG, V.D., Commanded 7th Inf. Bde., AIF 1915/17,6th Inf. Bde., AIF 1917/18. Merchant of Newcastle, NSW, b. Newcastle, 18 Nov. 1867.

Chapter 4

THE READINESS IS ALL

"If it be not now, yet it will come-the readiness is all..."

(Shakespeare *Hamlet*, Act V, Scene ii)

When war broke Charles Bingham Elwell was as ready as just about anyone. Ready, but lacking wartime experience. He had been highly trained by the Royal Navy and was a skilled and well-liked instructor. Charles now had the responsibilities of a command position as Lieutenant-Commander in charge of Royal Navy Reservists who was an integral part of the Australian Naval and Military Expeditionary Force (AN&MEF). He took his role as a leader quite seriously and was determined to look after the welfare of his men. On a personal level Charles Elwell had also taken on another role. He had become engaged. Little however, is known of his fiancée.

Medicine was the chosen career path for Brian Colden Antill Pockley. He had graduated as a qualified medical practitioner from Sydney University in March, 1914 and was working at nearby Sydney Hospital. Whilst at university he had been a Lieutenant in the University's regiment. This situation was in keeping with the military background of his forebears. It was not long before Brian showed his ability with the rifle as both his friends and instructors regarded him as a "crack" shot. At the same time, Dr. Brian Pockley was developing as a dedicated and conscientious doctor; a man always who did the best he could for those in his care.

Relevant to Pockley's involvement with the regiment was the introduction, in 1903, of a system of compulsory military training. The new nation of Australia had adopted in principle a system, based on the Swiss model, whereby military training was to be introduced through cadet units in schools and continued until the trainee had reached the mid-twenties. However this system did not come into existence until 1911. In that same year the Duntroon Military College was established.

Compulsory Military training on a part-time basis was linked with compulsory military service for home defence in times of war. Service overseas was to be on a voluntary basis. To the north "overseas" was defined as anywhere just north of the southern edge of New Guinea. Apparently there was considerable public resistance and non-compliance to these regulations but for the majority there was the feeling that such measures may well be warranted.

There were no such misgivings and little hesitation for Brian Pockley. He applied to join the AN&MEF on 17 August 1914 and was immediately appointed as a Captain in the Australian Army Medical Corps. This was less than a week after enlistment for military service began. Those in authority apparently considered his training in the University regiment was adequate. Two days after Brian Pockley enlisted he, along with other AN&MEF volunteers, left Sydney onboard HMAS *Berrima* bound for Rabaul and an unknown destiny.

William Miller took some time to recover from the appendix removal he had undergone in 1908. This meant that he was often out of work as recurrent bouts of pain made it difficult for him to move about

Captain Brian Colden Antill Pockley
AWM: H19316

freely. During such times he was dependent on his parents and spent considerable time at their small house in Redfern. Slowly he regained his strength and began to once again help out wherever he could gain remuneration.

A change in William's circumstances had come about in 1910. An old friend of his father's made contact with the family and during the visit he mentioned that there was work to be had back in the north-western areas of the state. One form of work which was of particular interest was that of droving. A succession of indifferent seasons mixed in with some good seasons had meant that sheep owners were keen to put their stock out to "the long paddock" in order to fatten them. Drovers, and especially those with cooking experience, were often in demand.

William made the slow journey back to Armidale. From there he set off towards Bourke. He made his base in the very small town of Byrock and soon gained work as a drover. Here he was back in his element. Though he was away from his family he was back in the

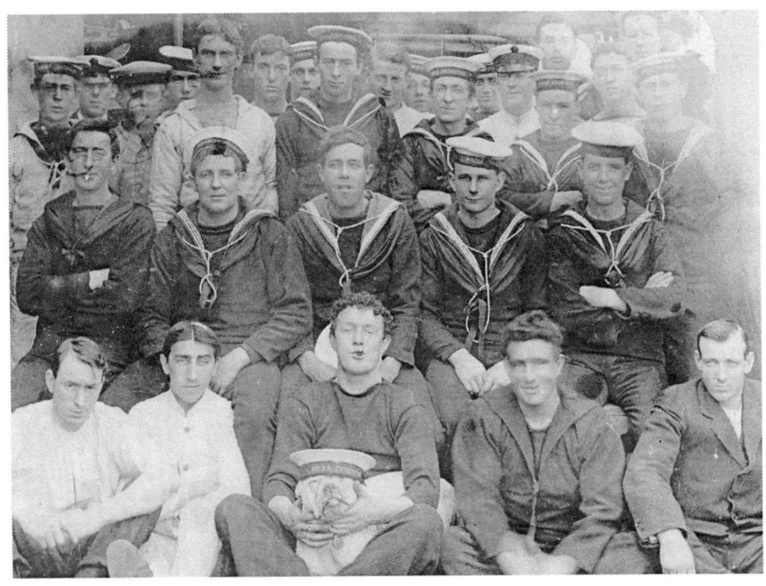

William Miller (front row, right) and '*Encounter* Shipmates'
Courtesy of Miller and Ellis families.

Australian bush; a place with which he was very familiar. William Miller travelled around the Bourke and Byrock areas quite blissfully unconcerned about the political storm clouds building up over Europe.

There was no military-style discipline in William's life. He was ruled only by the needs of the sheep he cared for; his hours were not fixed other than by the rising and setting of the sun. Nor was he advancing his formal education. His school was the school of the outdoors. However he was able to hone his cooking skills, learn to get on with the very few people he met and develop his own resourcefulness.

William found the summer of 1912 a particularly challenging one. It was very hot and after a few years away from his family he found that he was in need of re-establishing contact even if only briefly. He did not make it back to Sydney for Christmas but saved enough money to commence travel just prior to the new year. On his way, he spent some time in Armidale with his brother George, before continuing on his journey.

Arriving in Sydney in the first week of January 1913 William soon caught up with his parents, his old friends and the employers who had occasionally provided him with an income. His mother was delighted to see him and even more pleased with the fact that he had become an even better cook. After a time he was able to gain work as a labourer on the NSW railways which radiated out from Central station, opened just six years earlier.

William's work took him to the south down the track heading towards Melbourne. He ended up in Williamstown, a suburb of Melbourne, which was under-going rapid development as a shipping port. It was here that the American "Great White Fleet" had visited in 1908.

William was restless and looking for new adventures. As a result he made a momentous decision. A decision which was to substantially alter the course of his life for the next several years. William Miller decided to enlist in the newly formed Royal Australian Navy. At that time he had been living at the less than luxurious Port Phillip Hotel in Williamstown.

This decision was the result not only of his personal circumstances but also the result of developments occurring in Australia at that time. In the period from 1909 to 1910 under Prime Minister Fisher Australia took its first steps towards developing a fleet. There was also the formation of an agreement with Britain that Australia should have full control of its vessels during peacetime but during a time of war control would transfer to the Imperial authorities. In March 1913 a Naval college was setup and a site was chosen at Jervis Bay. The new navy was to be known as "The Royal Australian Navy" and her ships were to be designated "Her Majesty's Australian Ships" (HMAS).

On 24th February, 1913 William Miller enlisted in the Royal Australian Navy for a three-year term. His Naval records note the fact that he was five foot and six and three-quarter inches tall with grey eyes and a fresh complexion. They also note the existence of a large appendicitis scar. He was posted to HMAS *Encounter* as an Officer's Steward. (1)

On 21st June, 1913 the battlecruiser HMAS *Australia* was commissioned in Portsmouth, England. She then sailed from England in the company of the light cruiser, HMAS *Sydney* reaching Jervis Bay on 2nd October, 1913 where they were joined by the cruisers *Encounter* and *Melbourne*, the destroyers *Warrego, Parramatta* and *Yarra*. Two days later the fleet got underway and sailed up and into

Sydney Harbour where it was enthusiastically welcomed by the people of Sydney. William Miller was on board HMAS *Encounter.*

Over the next ten months, William Miller and his shipmates underwent extensive training in all aspects of naval training onboard HMAS *Encounter*. This training was conducted within Australian waters, generally in close proximity to the eastern seaboard. It was closely supervised by experienced officers of the Royal Navy. It is feasible, but not definitely known, that one of those officers was Charles Bingham Elwell. Although designated as an Officer's Steward, William also had to learn how to perform all duties, from operating *Encounter's* guns to swabbing her decks. Occasional shore breaks were welcomed. As it turned out these were to be few and far between once war broke out in August, 1914.

At the actual time of the declaration of war the *Encounter* was heading for Sydney. After a brief period of making ready, it was dispatched to the Port Moresby area accompanying other Australian naval vessels on what was, essentially, a reconnaissance mission. For William Miller, his time in the tropics, from 15th to 21st August, 1914, was a vastly new experience. Even at that time of year the weather was greatly different to that of Armidale, NSW. The *Encounter* then travelled south to meet up with the recently embarked AN&MEF who were about to undergo land-based training.

Also relevant is the culmination of Mawson's epic Antarctic expedition that occurred earlier in 1913. This expedition had been possible as a result of a concerted amount of fund raising. Heavily involved in that fund raising, but not in the expedition itself, was its expeditionary Secretary, one Conrad Constantine Eitel.[1] As Secretary

1 Cpl.C.C.Eitel (No.45 AN&MEF), Journalist of Sydney, born Neutral Bay, NSW, 1880. Also see second last chapter.

of the Expedition for eighteen months he had had sole control over all its funds.

Of German heritage, Conrad Eitel was now residing in Neutral Bay Sydney and worked as a journalist. He decided to enlist in the AN&MEF and went on to play a significant role in future events. He later undertook a course of action which would in turn attract the attention of his former journalist colleagues. For now he was just one of a number of men about to go off to war…

These men came from a wide variety of backgrounds with many vocations being represented:

"School teacher and wharf labourer, bank clerk and bushman, shop assistant and farrier stood side by side on the parade ground, waiting for the medical examination…There were those who, drifting without moorings in the ebb and flow of city life clutched at this chance of a new career… some were lured by a spirit of adventure… there were men who could turn their hands to everything, and there were men who had special technical or professional qualifications and experience." (2).

Among the earliest volunteers were two brothers with an impeccable educational background and whose father had considerable status within Sydney society. Charles Edye Manning[2] and his younger brother, Guy Owen Manning[3] were the sons of Charles James Manning and his second wife, Emily. Charles Manning Snr was a respected Sydney Barrister who at various times was a Supreme Court judge, a

2 Major CE Manning, 24th Btn. AIF, Barrister-at-law of Hunters Hill, NSW, born Hunters Hill, 24 Oct. 1879. Killed in action France, 7 August, 1916.

3 Capt.GO Manning, Plantation Manager of Papua, born Hunters Hill, NSW 4 Nov. 1881. Accidentally killed Myom, New Ireland, 18 June, 1915

Council member of The King's School and a fellow of the Senate of the University of Sydney. (3)

Not surprisingly the two brothers attended The Kings School as boarders where Charles distinguished himself by being joint dux in 1897 as well as gaining places in the First XV and the 1st Shooting team. Charles followed his father into Law, was a practising Barrister

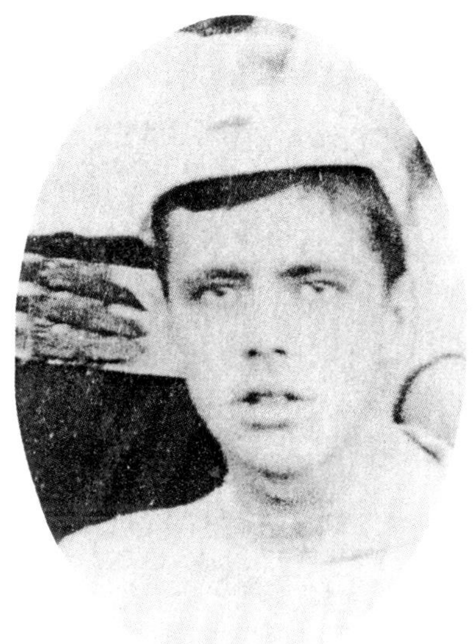

Charles Manning
Courtesy of The King's School, Parramatta

at the time of enlistment and was immediately appointed to the rank of Lieutenant. Less is known about the academic achievements of his brother Guy, who went on to pursue a career path quite somewhat removed from that of Charles. Guy's occupation when he enlisted a few days before Charles, was given as "plantation manager". (4)

Nonetheless both brothers were to prove very useful to the tasks and problems which arose later in New Guinea, but in different ways.

The outcome of their involvement in the events of World War I did, however, have a similarity as will become apparent later.

The Manning brothers were schoolmates with Charles Elwell however they were probably not close friends as their ages differed slightly and Elwell was not a boarding student. They were now onboard different vessels, heading for the same destination. Destiny had once more thrown them together…

The men assembled at Victoria Barracks in Sydney and then marched to the nearby Agricultural Showground where they were medically assessed. Initially they were sworn in to serve anywhere, on land or sea, for an unlimited period. However they were sworn in again with a new form a week later. This time the volunteers agreed to service outside Australia but for a definite period which was stated as six months. (5) Similar assemblies and embarkations of men in the AN&MEF were taking places in other centres, notably Melbourne and Adelaide.

Of those who enlisted, very few belonged to the Commonwealth Military Forces and so the majority had to be clothed, armed and equipped. Colonel Holmes received his appointment on 10th August, 1914 and the speed with which he took on his task was such that within a matter of days the infantry was ready to go abroad. Equipped they may have been; trained for battle in the tropics they weren't. The training was to come later.

On Tuesday 18th August, 1914 the men of Sydney were marched along Oxford, College and Macquarie Streets on their way to Fort Macquarie, currently the site of the Sydney Opera House. Thousands lined the streets to cheer them on their way. Girls threw colourful ribbons in the manner of a modern day ticker-tape parade.

A proud Mother and her Son
AWM H11567

Relatives and friends of the men greeted them. Some, at least for a time, marched alongside their departing heroes.

Once at Fort Macquarie the men boarded two Sydney ferries for Cockatoo Island and from there to the former Peninsula and Oriental branch liner, *Berrima* which had been chartered as a troop transport and was later commissioned as an auxiliary cruiser.

Colonel Holmes pointed out to the Chief of General Staff, Colonel Legge, that the raising of this force had been formed more quickly than their combined efforts to gather together in raising a smaller group of military personnel back in 1900 during the Boer War. Whilst Legge may have agreed with Holmes, the Minister for Defence, Senator Millen, did not. In a meeting with Holmes, Senator Millen chastised Holmes for taking so long. Holmes was almost at a loss for words...

Once on board Captain Brian Pockley found that he had a two-berth cabin to himself but one which lacked a porthole. He did however point out that men were to "sleep in hammocks pretty closely slung and will be much worse off." Even though they were on board "a very steady old boat" there were already a few men who were seasick to whom he had to tend. (5).

Early enlistments in the AN&MEF
AWM H19498

Conrad Eitel, writing for *The Sydney Morning Herald* shared similar views to Captain Pockley on the accommodation provided for the men. He reported that each man was allotted:

"a small space in which to stow his marching kit, rifle and kit-bag…each man has a canvas hammock…with hammocks swung so closely together that if a man fell out of his hammock he would fall into another…Five hundred men cooped up in a confined space make it pretty murky…Not one man imagines that this is a picnic." (6)

HMAS *Berrima* set out of Sydney Harbour on 19th August and as no destination had been announced there was considerable interest in noting in which direction the vessel headed as it cleared the Sydney Heads. As the vessel set off towards the north, opinions that the expedition was heading for German colonial possessions in the western Pacific, were seemingly confirmed. Two days later anchor was dropped in Moreton Bay but the men were denied shore leave. This was not a popular decision among the men but they accepted it. Rebellion was to raise its head more prominently later, but not among the men of the AN&MEF.

Meanwhile William Miller was on board HMAS *Encounter* attending to the officers. This vessel had been ordered to join the supply ship *Aorangi,* the submarine tenders *Protector* and *Upolu,* the submarines *AE1* and *AE2* at a rendezvous at Palm Island, north of Townsville and inside the Great Barrier Reef. He too, although he did have by now his "sea legs", was himself getting used to a new situation; no longer was he on a training exercise; this was the real thing.

During the voyage north the men on board the *Berrima* were drilled as much as possible as the limited space allowed. Captain Pockley was kept busy treating those men who had to gain their sea-legs. Much of his time was spent administering to men suffering seasickness at various levels. A quick recovery was essential as they were about to be subjected to a much more vigorous regime and in a hot and sweaty climate with which most of them were unfamiliar.

Chapter 5

SHAPING UP: TRAINING AND PREPARATIONS

"Force without Wisdom falls of its own weight."

(Horace)

Looking back over the backgrounds of the men of the AN&MEF it is easy to conclude that the officers were men from privileged backgrounds with assured futures whilst those they led were less well-educated and concerned with daily routines and more simple pleasures. The officers were doing their duty, in support of the Empire; their men were seeking adventure, motivated by personal desire for money and excitement. Whilst there is more than a scrap of truth in that assessment there were exceptions to the rule.

However once they had departed Australia, the men of the AN&MEF, were all thrown together "in the one boat", both figuratively and literally. Most could guess, but did not know for sure, where they were bound; few had any experience with the climate and conditions of that region and few had any real military experience.

It may have been easy for the likes of Colonel Holmes to remain aloof from, yet concerned about his men, but for Brian Pockley,

Charles Elwell and William Miller circumstances were considerably different and to varying degrees for each of them. As a member of the Australian Army Medical Corps, Brian Pockley mingled with the men as he performed his medical duties. Compassion for them was to become his prime concern and he proved to be most diligent. Charles Elwell was also involved with his subordinates on a personal level as he went about his duties as an officer and a trainer but always kept a certain distance from them; familiarity breeds contempt. William Miller, by virtue of his role as both a steward and a seaman, mixed with both the officers and the other ranks but the nature of his personal contact with each group differed greatly. He had to tread a careful path.

Aside from any altruistic national aspirations or personal hopes for glory and adventure, what of the immediate goal which all men of the AN&MEF sought? Was their goal a worthy one? Few expected that lives would be lost but was it worth the effort, the long and difficult journey?

It is worthwhile briefly assessing the situation in German New Guinea in 1914, especially, Rabaul, the centre of administration. It is also essential to evaluate the readiness of the German enemy. They were in little doubt that they would soon be under attack once war had been declared...

Although suffering the impact of some unusually dry seasons, Rabaul, the capital of the German colonial possessions in New Guinea, was quite an attractive place in 1914. It sat in well-protected Blanche Bay within Simpson Harbour and was surrounded by an impressive array of steep-sided green mountains. One of the earliest German commercial contacts with the area had been that of the firm Goddefroy and Sons which had set up a trading post in the nearby Duke of York Islands in the 1870s.

German New Guinea troops in training
AWM: A02544

The first attempt at colonisation of the Bismarck Archipelago came in 1879 when a group of some eighty European settlers, forty of whom were German, arrived in the area. However the site they chose was a poor choice as malaria there proved to be entrenched and the local natives were very hostile. Within just a few years this colony was abandoned with most of the survivors leaving for Noumea. The most significant commercial activities in the area were those developed by one Emma Forsayth. Born in Samoa, she was the daughter of the American Consul and a Samoan princess. She later deserted her Scottish husband, James, and became involved with an Australian adventurer by the name of Thomas Farrell. Initially establishing themselves in the Duke of York Islands they later moved to the Rabaul area and set up the first coconut plantation in German New Guinea.

Somewhat of a character, Emma became widely known as Queen Emma. Slowly but surely German commercial activities (trading and plantation agriculture) began to increase.

The German government really only became interested in the area after it had annexed the north-eastern part of the mainland and the Bismarck Archipelago (1884) and when it realised its potential as base for a wireless station. Yet, according to S. S. MacKenzie, the writer of Volume X of C.E.W. Bean's history of World War I, no wireless station existed at Rabaul until July, 1914, the month prior to the outbreak of the war. Prior to then, unless a German cruiser lay in the harbour there was no wireless contact between Rabaul and the outside world. In that month a temporary wireless station was established at Bitapaka, just inland from Kabakaul. It was through this station that Rabaul learnt of the outbreak of war. (1)

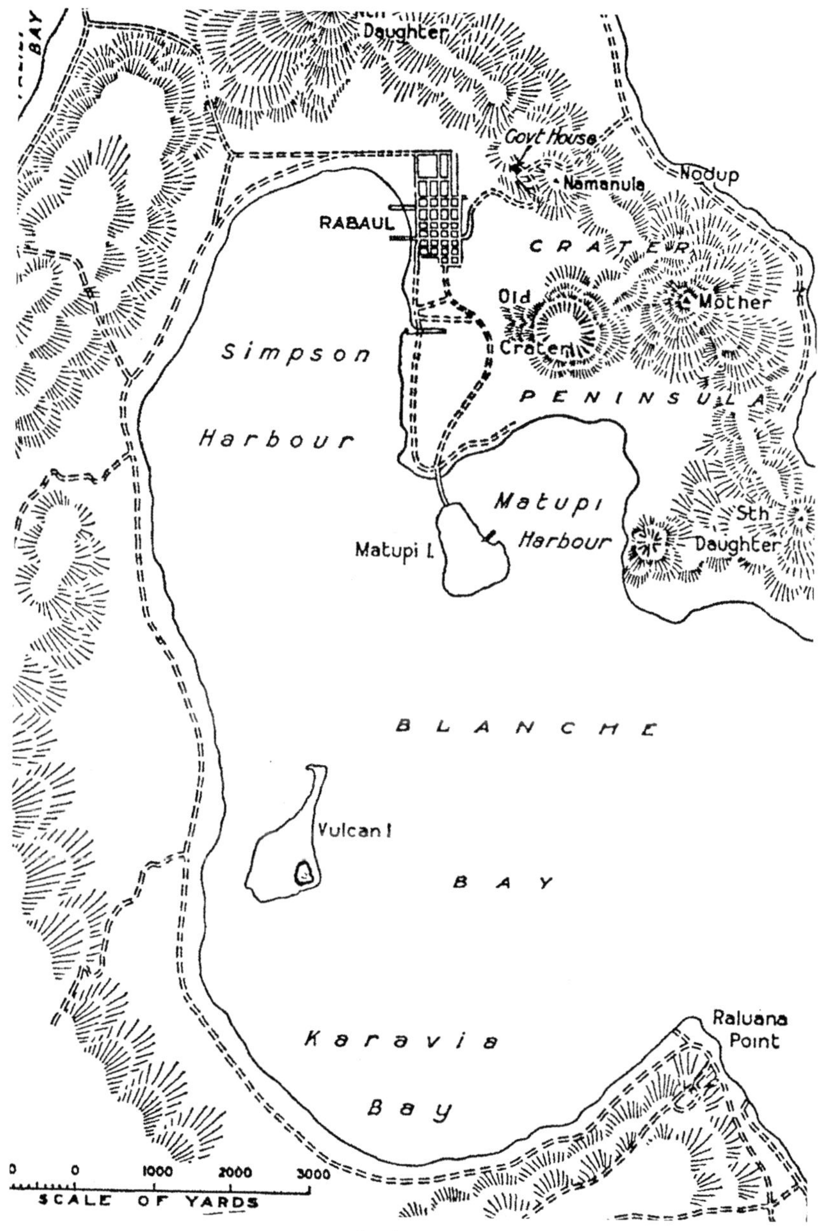

Rabaul Area
Official History of WWI – C.E.W. Bean

Germany makes ready

At the time of the arrival of news of the outbreak of hostilities, 5th August,1914, the Acting Governor, Dr. Haber, was away on a visit to the mainland of New Guinea. Because of the need to take precautions as British warships were in the area it was not until some nine days later that Dr. Haber was able to arrive safely back in Rabaul. Here he was to learn that on 12th August the Australian destoyers *Yarra, Parramatta* and *Warrego* had entered Simpson Harbour and Matupi Harbour (both of which lie in Blanche Bay). Men from HMAS *Warrego* had come ashore and had destroyed the telephones and telegraphic equipment at the nearby post offices.

In the meantime steps had already been taken to deal with what the Germans believed was inevitable…an attack on their base. The first precaution taken had been to transfer the centre of administration from Rabaul to Toma which was inland from Herbertshohe. This precaution had been taken even before the return of Dr. Haber.

The German Colonial Office had planned this for some time. They realised that the small settlements of Rabaul and Herbertshohe could not hold out against an enemy squadron. They reasoned that so long as the German Navy was able to gain and maintain control in the sea of the western Pacific it would be unlikely for the British to begin a protracted attack on the wireless station, particularly if it were made less accessible.

A second precaution, taken at the same time, was to dispose of German government Treasury funds and stores. These were distributed among the German commercial concerns and a cash reserve of 186,293 marks was sent on to Toma. The recovery of these funds was to become a secondary goal for the Australians.

The Germans readied their few military forces. Day reservists of the German army were called up for service and told to report to the heights above Simpson Harbour for training.

It was the wireless station which was the prime concern of the Germans. It was decided to proceed with haste in the construction of the permanent wireless station at Bitapaka so that the temporary one currently there could be moved inland. This too, was later moved to the area near Toma. When the men from the *Warrego* had questioned the German District Officer at Rabaul they had been told that there was no wireless station within fifty miles of Rabaul. They knew this to be a lie but what they didn't realise was that such German militia as was available had been deployed to Bitapaka to protect the wireless station.

All of these precautions were carried out in August, 1914 and so by 9th September the new, inland wireless station had been established. Unfortunately, for the Germans, it was not fully operational as the receiving equipment was defective.

At the same time as they were transferring their centre of administration out of Rabaul, the Germans were also establishing an observation post nearby. The chosen site was an extinct volcano known as "Mother" to Europeans; to the natives it was "Kombiu". Located to the east of, and some six hundred metres above Rabaul, this peak gave a commanding view of St. George's Channel, Blanche Bay and the coast to the south.

Towards the middle of August, 1914 the Germans at Rabaul were becoming concerned about the Australian Naval presence in the area.

On two occasions a small number of British subjects living in Rabaul were detained on suspicion that they were attempting to communicate by way of manual signals. On each occasion they were released soon after apart from one Frederick Jolley[1] who they would not allow to return to his plantation as it was too close to the new German headquarters. He was instead sent to a settlement in New Ireland with instructions that he be properly treated. (2)

It would be true to say that the size of the German military force in no way matched that of the approaching AN&MEF so the Germans were hopeful that their Navy would gain dominance in the area. If this became the case then the continued existence of their wireless station was significant. To this effect, they deployed their troops to two key locations.

The wireless station at Bitapaka was occupied by eight white and sixty native officers under the command of Captain Wuchert. If the pressure on them from a landing force became too great they were to destroy the wireless station and retreat to Tobera. Another company of ten white and one hundred and forty native soldiers under the command of Lieutenant Mayer was stationed at Herbertshohe (later changed to "Kokopo"). If forced to they were to retire towards Toma. As they withdrew they would be monitored by men occupying two separate observation posts in the Toma area.

The Germans had taken other much more sinister precautions to protect the newly established wireless station at Toma. They had planted explosives under the road to Bitapaka.The men of the AN&MEF were to learn about these measures as they moved inland from Bitapaka.

1 Later Captain F.R.Jolley, 4th and 58th Bns, AIF, b. Prahan, Vic., 3 January, 1883.

Training for tropical conditions

The ships carrying the men of the AN&MEF spent more than a week anchored off Palm Island. This time was put to good use. Each day the men were taken ashore where they were drilled in manoeuvres and taught how to stay in touch with each other when in thickly-wooded country. This was designed to stand them in good stead in the jungles of New Guinea. A rifle range was set up and used to train the men in proper use of their rifles.

Palm Island, September 1914; Returning from training
AWM: PO3078 003

This period of intense training was vital for two major reasons. The recruitment and kitting-out process had been done so quickly that virtually no time at all had been made available for training in military discipline and use of weapons. Many of the men had no background in these areas. In addition there was a very real need to provide at least some means by which the men could become acclimatised to tropical conditions. Later experiences were to support the view that New Guinea was a place best suited to men aged from about their early twenties to their late thirties. Only experienced and fit men could be expected to endure prolonged marching and fighting under the energy-sapping conditions that awaited them.

It should also be noted that the German military personnel based in New Guinea, though small in number, were at an advantage in both these key areas of training and acclimatisation. However good progress was made by the new recruits. Even the rawest among them learnt how to handle a rifle expertly. By the time the men again put to sea it was felt that they were capable of putting up as good a fight as could be expected of them. But they were yet to be tested.

On the other hand there were some reservations felt about the training undertaken by the naval contingent. Many of them had never before put to sea and much of their training was left up to junior officers, rather than those who would lead them into battle. The Naval reservists were, however, given frequent practice in landing troops from boats. Future events were to show that the concerns were unfounded.

On 2nd September the *Sydney, Encounter, Berrima* and *Aorangi* set off for Port Moresby. They were followed two days later by the *Upolu,* the *Protector* and the submarines *AE1* and *AE2.* At Port Moresby they met up with HMAS *Sydney,* HMAS *Parramatta* HMA Transport *Kanowna.* This last vessel carried a contingent of 500 volunteers from northern Queensland, known as the Kennedy Regiment. Holmes inspected these troops and was extremely disappointed with the result. He found that he had before him a commander with inadequate military training, no regimental staff and relatively inexperienced officers. Moreover, the ship's company had not been consulted about the expectation that they

Capt. Hugh Quinn
AWM: H17225

would take the vessel well beyond its authorised run, and so were ready to go on strike.

A mutiny of sorts did in fact occur. On 7th September the fleet left Port Moresby for Rossel Island (to the east) when it was soon noticed that the *Kanowna* was falling behind. HMAS *Sydney* was sent back to investigate. It was found that the firemen had mutinied but several AN&MEF volunteers had taken over the stoking. Holmes made the immediate decision to send the *Kanowna* back to Townsville and have the unit disbanded and subsequently reorganised. He informed Admiral Patey of his decision. Admiral Patey agreed that there were sufficient men aboard the *Berrima* to complete the assigned mission.

The men aboard the *Kanowna* were the victim of circumstances beyond their control. They were willing to go ahead with the task and would have stoked the fires all the way to Rabaul. The men were bitterly disappointed. Many of them later joined the AIF and served in places such as Gallipoli. Two such men were Captain H. Quinn and Lieutenant H.P. Armstrong, both killed at Quinn's Post Gallipoli.

Once the fleet had gathered at Rossel Island a council of war was held to discuss plans for the attack on German New Guinea. Final plans were drawn up by Colonel Holmes, Admiral Patey[2], Captain Glossop[3] of HMAS *Sydney* and Commander Stevenson[4] of HMAS *Berrima*. Admiral Patey issued an operational order for the occupation of Rabaul and Herbertshohe.

The plan was for the *Sydney* accompanied by the destroyers to proceed to Simpson Harbour (adjacent to Rabaul) where the *Sydney* was to attack any German ships there. If none were there she was to remain outside the harbour while the destroyers were to enter it and deal with any smaller enemy ships inside the harbour.

All of those on board the *Berrima* were made ready. Captain Pockley and the medical staff became extremely busy. A second vaccination for enteric fever was given to the men and a first to the men of the naval unit who had not previously been vaccinated in Sydney. Vaccinations against smallpox were also administered and quinine was made available. The clothing for the soldiers included a khaki cotton

2 Admiral Sir George E Patey, K.CMG, K.C.V.O R.N C-in-C. Royal Australian Fleet, 1913/15, North America & West Indies Station 1915/16, b.Plymouth, England, 24 Feb.1859.

3 Vice-Admiral JCT Glossop C.B. R.N., b.Twickenham, England, 23 Oct. 1871.

4 Rear-Admiral JB Stevenson, CMG,R.N. (later R.A.N.), b.Liverpool,England 7 Aug. 1876.

working dress but predominantly their uniforms were of wool which proved to be unbearable in the tropical heat. Despite this Holmes was able to report that the men were in high spirits:

"There is a most excellent feeling on board; the discipline is of the best, food is good, and there is not a single case in hospital...the work on which I am engaged is of great importance to the Empire and will be of historical value in changing, if ever so little, the face of the map, it will, as far as I can see, be carried out without a shot being fired, which will be a keen disappointment to many with me, who, like young foxhounds, would be all the better as soldiers if they were blooded." (3)

Strong words indeed! The attack was to take place in the early hours of Friday, 11th September, 1914.

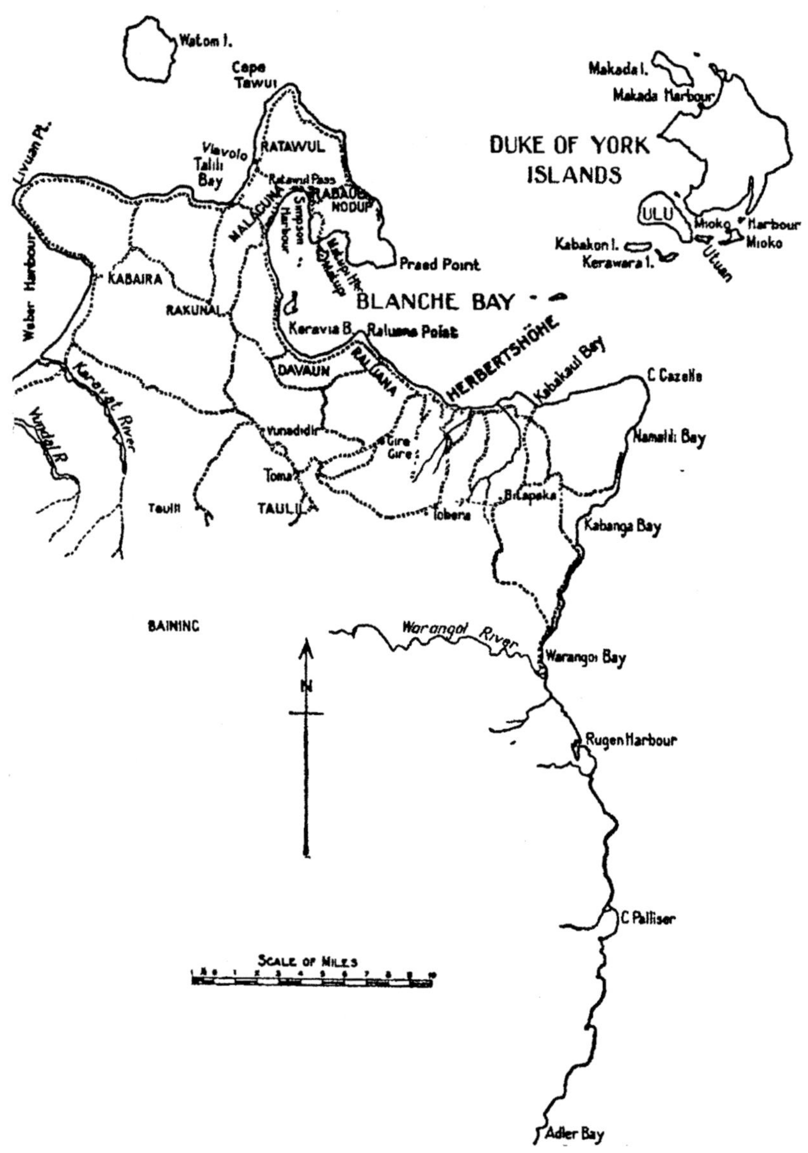

NE German New Guinea
(Official History of WWI - C.E.W. Bean)

Chapter 6

INTO BATTLE

Cry 'Havoc' and let slip the dogs of War

(Shakespeare, *Julius Caesar*, Act III, Scene i)

Plan of attack

Admiral Patey and Colonel Holmes agreed that both Rabaul and Herbertshohe had to be taken and garrisoned. The military contingent was to land at Rabaul, the administrative centre, whilst the Herbertshohe garrison was to be drawn from the Naval Brigade under the command of Commander Beresford[1]. Detachments from the force travelled inland to search for any other wireless stations.

Preliminary reconnaissance had earlier been made of Blanche Bay to ensure that it was empty of enemy ships and to allow HMAS *Parramatta* to assess the suitability of the Rabaul jetty for use by HMAS *Berrima*. Meanwhile HMAS *Sydney* was to transfer 50 of the naval contingent (who had previously been transferred from the *Berrima* at Port Moresby). Twenty-five of these men were to go onboard the *Warrego* and *Yarra* for transport to Kabakaul (four miles or seven kilometres east of Herbertshohe) and the other twenty-five to be landed at Herbertshohe itself.

1 Commander J.A.H.Beresford: RAN, of Melbourne, b. Langharne, Wales 11 August, 1861.

On guard, outside the broad area of Blanche Bay HMAS *Encounter* patrolled the area near Cape Tawui to the north whilst the two submarines, *AE1* and *AE2* were stationed at Cape Gazelle to the south.

Reconnaissance

The task of assessing the strength of the German defences was assigned to the Royal Australian Navy. Beginning at 3.30 on the morning of Friday 11 September, 1914, the first parry was carried out by HMAS *Sydney* in conjunction with the three Australian destroyers, *Warrego, Parramatta* and *Yarra.* With the *Sydney* standing guard the destroyers entered Simpson and Matupi Harbours on a reconnaissance mission. They found these areas empty of enemy ships.

A few hours later HMAS *Australia,* the *Encounter* and the *Berrima* approached the area of Herbertshohe. HMAS *Parramatta* conducted an examination of the pier at Rabaul whilst picket boats were used to sweep for mines. No mines were found anywhere. Also nearby were other naval vessels including HMAS *Australia,* the storeship *Aorangi* and the two submarines *AE1* and *AE2.*

Lieutenant-Commander Elwell was on board the *Berrima* and Captain Pockley had five days earlier been placed onboard HMAS *Sydney.* It was from this vessel that Brian Pockley penned a letter to his family:

"I… am attached to Lieutenant Bowen and 50 of the RAN Reserve. The ship is cleared for action at present and is accompanied by the three destroyers... I have just come out of the ship's surgery. It is 95 deg. there.

"I do not think it will matter now to tell you that our objective tomorrow is Rabaul and Herbertshohe in New Britain. We will make a night attack at 3am tonight. Probably there will be no opposition at all.

"Our objective is a wireless station close to Herbertshohe. One 4 miles away and the other about 7 or 8. We are not even certain that they exist, and much doubt that they are defended. However we shall see tomorrow... I am the only medical officer with the party and have one private. We shall each accompany one of the wireless station parties. Of course it is just possible that we may meet with naval opposition in entering the harbour, but if we do you will either hear all about it from Prevost or else you won't get this letter. Personally I think it will be a very pleasant little picnic...

Much love to you all,

Brian." (1)

Brian Pockley had sounded somewhat of an ominous tone when he had mentioned the possibility of his parents of not getting his letter. His statement about him attending a pleasant picnic was not borne out by what was to come...

Charles Elwell may not have been writing a letter to his parents in these the few hours remaining before he could be asked to go into battle for the first time. Yet the gravity of the approaching events was weighing heavily on his mind. He was not designated as the leader of the men to be sent ashore from the *Berrima*. This role had been given to his colleague and friend Lieutenant-Commander Gillam[2]. It was

2 Lt.-Comm.,O.W.Gillam; V.D., RANR, Shipping Agent and Merchant of Newcastle, NSW; b. Albany, WA, 26 July, 1877.

intended that Elwell remain on board with the men under his charge.

The night before the landing Lieutenant-Commander Elwell had just written to his fiancée when he offered his writing pad to Gillam. Many years later Gillam was to recall the following, rather disturbing conversation:

"Take it as a keepsake old chap for I'll never want it again."

I said, "What do you mean you old goat—you don't even land tomorrow."

He said, "I'll worry Beresford until he lets me land with you."

I said. "You're morbid—come and have a drink."

Gillam said that he mentioned this conversation to others at the time. He was then to notice something else happen which he also saw as rather strange and in fact some sort of premonition.

Rations were being handed out as the men were about to go ashore. Gillam was busy seeing that his men received all that they needed when he turned around in time to see Elwell transferring his cheese and biscuits to Gillam's empty haversack. Elwell had convinced Beresford to allow him to accompany Gillam and his men. When Gillam protested about Elwell's giving away his food Elwell replied:

"You'll want them old chap. I never will." (2)

It is with reported conversations such as these that create dilemnas for any later reader. Did Charles Elwell have some sort of premonition of what was to come? It may simply be the case that Charles Elwell had other writing paper and also did not anticipate that he would become hungry...

William Miller was on board HMAS *Encounter,* too busy attending to his normal duties as an officer's steward to think about writing to his parents Annie and George. The *Encounter* was getting underway ready for its delegated patrol to the waters north of Blanche Bay. It was not the intention of those in charge that either he or any other member of the ship's crew would take a direct part in the onshore activities about to unfold. Nonetheless, the *Encounter* was not destined to be a non-participating bystander.

Landing Site — Kabakaul Jetty
AWM: H17182

First Australian attack of World War I

At 6am the *Australia* entered Karavia Bay. One hour later 25 Petty officers and men under the command of Lieutenant Bowen[3] and Midshipman Buller[4] were landed on a jetty a little to the east of Kabakaul pier. Accompanying them was Captain Brian Pockley of the Australian Army Medical Corps.

They possessed no map of the area and found themselves surrounded by a few houses near the jetty. The Australians were able to learn from the resident Chinese and natives that the Germans had retreated inland down a nearby quite well-formed road. As he was about to set off Bowen was reinforced by a further 10 men led by Gunners Yeo[5] and Bacon. He decided to use them as his liaison with the beach as he and the landing party moved inland.

Lieutenant Bowen employed a method of advance which was to be frequently used by Australian troops later during World War II when Australians again fought an enemy in New Guinea. He directed his men to stay off the road and he used scouts to move ahead of the main body. This method served him well until they passed the crossroad with the road leading to Herbertshohe and entered a plantation area. Beyond this plantation was dense scrub which forced them to divert to the west until the scrub thinned again.

3 Commr R.G. Bowen; RAN, of Melbourne, b. Taggarty, VIC., 14 January, 1879.

4 Lieut.-Commr. R.L. Buller; RANR, Public Servant of Moonee Ponds, VIC., b. Geelong, Vic., 21 May, 1894.

5 Lieut,-Commr., S.T.P. Yeo; RN, of Stoke, England, b. Devonshire, 7 Sept., 1884.

L-R: Col. Holmes, Lt. Col Watson, Col. Paton, Capt. Goodsell onboard HMAS *Berrima*
AWM: H12840

First Australian shot fired "in anger" in World War I

Soon after they returned to the area of the road one of the advance scouts, Petty Officer Palmer[6] noticed that they were being observed by a group of three Germans and about 20 native soldiers who were lying in ambush. As they were in a position to attack the main Australia party Palmer shot the German who he saw was possibly their leader.

This was the first shot fired "in anger" by Australian forces during World War 1. This shot set off a chain of repercussions as Palmer wounded Sergeant-Major Mauderer by shooting him in the hand. Palmer then escorted Mauderer to Lieutenant Bowen.

Bowen decided to take full advantage of this new development. He chose to use bluff. He commanded Mauderer to march ahead of the advancing Australians and to call out to his comrades that they may as well surrender as 800 Australians were advancing on them. Bowen's bluff worked as the rest of the party observed by Palmer now emerged from the jungle and surrendered.

It was later revealed that the Germans remaining at their headquarters were aware that only a force of some 30 men had been landed. As a result a small party had been dispatched to cut them off from any reinforcements. Somehow news of Bowen's bluff was relayed to Captain von Klewitz, the commander at Headquarters who convinced the German Governor to move further inland. As a consequence there was now a total breakdown of the German coastal defences.

None of this was known to Bowen. What he did know and appreciate was the fact that he now had in his possession maps of the

6 Petty Officer G.R. Palmer; RANR, Master Mariner of Parkville, Victoria; b. Essex, England, 16 Jan. 1879.

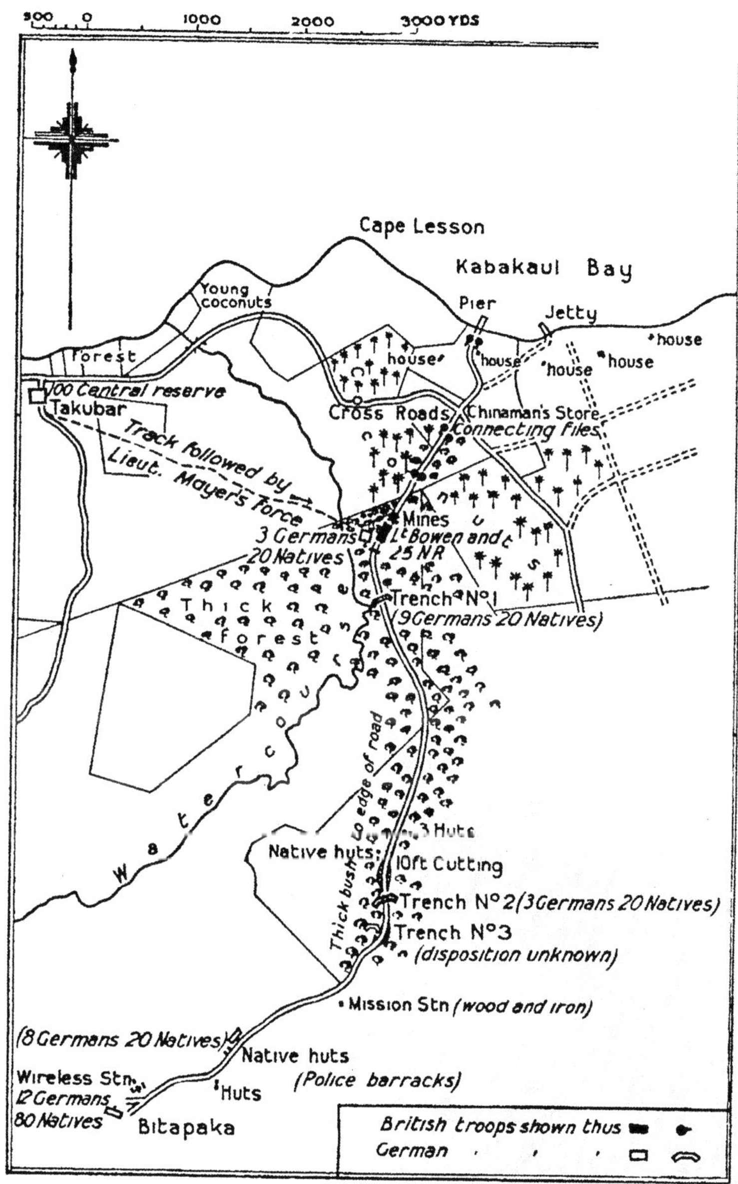

The Road to Bitapaka
(Official History of WWI – C.E.W. Bean)

Bitapaka road. He also knew that resistance had begun and so he sent Buller back to the coast with the three German prisoners and a request for reinforcements.

Rules of War

Also unknown to Bowen was the fact that in using a prisoner under threat in this manner he had unwittingly infringed the rules of war. In 1914 the Imperial government issued a Field Service Pocket Book which stated that prisoners can be given tasks but "nothing to do with military operations" (3).

Many years later, that very thorough historian, C.E.W.Bean investigated this incident with both S. S. MacKenzie and Robert Garran, Solicitor-General of the Attorney-General's department. The former believed that technically Bowen had infringed the rules of war but his actions were excusable on the grounds that his actions had saved a loss of life on both sides and also because, being early in the war, Bowen may well have been unaware of this rule. (4) Attorney-General Garran stated that the rule is expressed in very wide terms and therefore Bowen may, technically, have infringed the rules of war but, if so, the infringement was not a serious one. (5) At no stage was there ever any indication that the matter needed to be dealt with further. British military authorities declared they had no intention of taking the matter further. When Bowen himself became aware of their examination of the incident he too weighed in with his own opinion:

"I would imagine there were hundreds of cases in the early part of the war where self-preservation without dishonor would cause any person in command to exercise common sense…" (6).

Lieutenant Bowen was indeed a man who employed common sense as his later actions were to prove…

Upon arrival at the landing area Buller relayed Bowen's request for more men. Lieutenant Hill[7] was despatched with 59 men hurriedly brought ashore from the *Warrego* and the *Yarra*. Of these men only fourteen were armed with rifles; the rest were armed with pistols and cutlasses. Many of them, including Hill himself, were wearing incomplete uniforms, lacking the proper badges.

Whilst awaiting the arrival of these reinforcements, Bowen and his men moved further inland. Round a left-hand bend in the road they became aware of a German trench dug about 500 yards (450 metres) further on. Bowen had continued to deploy his men in two groups working in the scrub off to the side of the road. His men came under rifle fire from the enemy; most of this fire was coming from either the trench ahead or other rifle pits. For some time Bowen's men remained unharmed but at about 9.30am Able Seaman Billy Williams[8] was shot through the stomach. His companion, Stoker Kember, carried him back along the road.

Earlier Captain Pockley had reported to Lieutenant Bowen that Major Mauderer was suffering badly from a significant loss of blood. Pockley felt he had no alternative but to amputate Mauderer's hand… a painful process under trying conditions but one which Mauderer endured stoically. Captain Pockley had just finished this operation when he was made aware of the wounding of Williams. Bowen was

7 Lieut.-Commr., G.A. Hill; RNR (later RAN), Master Mariner of Coogee, NSW; b. Edgbaston, England, 1 May, 1880, died 4 May, 1931.

8 AB Seaman W.G.V. Williams; Melbourne City Council Employee, b. Richmond, Vic., 24 Nov., 1885, killed 11 September, 1914.

Position of landmine on
Bitapaka Road
AWM: H03288

aware that native soldiers were working their way amongst the Australian flanks and so he sent Able Seaman Annear[9] along with Pockley. According to Bowen, Williams was wounded at about 9.30am.

It took very little time for Captain Pockley to realise that Williams was seriously wounded and needed to be sent back to the rear. At this point he made two very fateful decisions. Pockley took off his own red-cross brassard and tied it to Stoker Kember's [10]hat. Kember, with the help of another, was to take Williams back to the shore. In doing this Captain Pockley was showing his concern for the men in his care. He was also removing any form of insignia which would identify himself as a non-combatant. It was to prove a caring but costly decision.

Captain Pockley, along with Annear turned back and began to advance once more down the road. Almost immediately they again came under fire and took shelter. They were still some distance behind Bowen and his men. After a short time Pockley instructed Annear to

9 Officer's Steward A.O. Annear; ,Shop Asst. of Elsternwick, Vic., b. Campbell's Creek, 26 Jan. 1893, died,31 Oct., 1925.

10 Leading Stoker W. Kember; of Canley Vale NSW, b. Scaynes Hill, Sussex England 22 August,1885.

remain where he was and again moved forward alone. He had walked about ten paces when he too was shot. Arrangements were made to transport the wounded Pockley back to the shore. Again, according to Lieutenant Bowen, Pockley was wounded at about 10.30am and was about 200 yards (190 metres) behind where Bowen was at that time. (7)

Both Captain Pockley and Able Seaman Williams were taken onboard HMAS *Berrima* and it was here that both of these men died that same afternoon. No one can say for sure which of the two died first. It would seem that AB Williams was wounded just before Captain Pockley. Suffice it to say that they were the first Australian fatalities of the Great War; one an Army officer, the other a Naval seaman.

Meanwhile Lieutenant Bowen and his men continued to move forward toward the German trench. They were trying to outflank them with the main group led by Bowen advancing from the left and another group of five men, led by Petty Officer Sandys,[11] approaching from the right. One party came upon a German crouching in a rifle pit. Again Bowen decided to move forward with his prisoner in front of him.

At about 9.50am they were joined by Lieutenant Hill and his variously-dressed crew. He and Bowen planned their attack on the German trench. It was decided that their forces would be divided into three groups; one to keep an eye on the trench whilst the other two tried to outflank and then attack it. Bowen proceeded to put this plan into effect; using his prisoner as a shield, he called upon the Germans to surrender. Receiving no response he pushed the prisoner aside and was then shot in the head.

Midshipman Buller ran to Bowen's aid and was able to carry him to safety on the side of the road. Bowen had enough presence of mind

11 Gunner F.R .Sandys; RN, b. Plaistow, Essex, England, 24 May, 1881.

to call out to Hill to take charge. He also noted that it was now about 10.10am. Once more Buller was sent back to summon reinforcements.

Allowances for such a situation had already been made. Commander Beresford was ordered to land another 100 men of the Naval contingent. He landed two companies and a machine-gun section; one company was hastily sent forward under the command of Lieutenant-Commander Charles Bingham Elwell. Not being sure exactly where Hill and his men were and yet keen to get to them quickly, Elwell decided to move his men through the bush but with patrols of six men moving down the road. Letters later written by the men sent down the road in this manner, indicate that it didn't take them long to realise that they had placed themselves in mortal danger. They quickly took cover by the side of the road and kept their heads down. The bush in front of them was almost impenetrable but they continued to move forward cautiously.

After moving forward in this manner for some 40 minutes his group suffered their first casualty. A sniper shot rang out claiming the life of twenty-nine year old Able Seaman John Courtney[12] from North Sydney. His real name was John Edward Walker and he had stuck to the pseudonym he once used when getting work on a ship. Courtney died almost instantly from two shots; one through the chest and the other through the base of his skull. He died at about 1pm; the precise time is not known but it is possible that he may have died even before Williams and Pockley.

As Elwell's men advanced they continued to come under enemy fire. Quite suddenly and almost by accident they encountered an unexpected obstacle. A seaman was startled when a New Guinea

12 AB Seaman J.E.Walker; RANR, (Served as J.Courtney), Stoker of Ross Island, Townsville,Qld., Killed in action, 11 Sept. 1914.

trooper emerged from behind a tree and tried to wrestle his gun from him. He was able to resist the native who he shot dead. It was then that the seaman noticed some wires at the base of the tree. Upon investigation the Australians found that the Germans had placed a mine underneath the road. The native trooper had been placed up the tree as a lookout.

The mine was quickly disconnected. However the location of the group of men involved here was all too obvious to the concealed enemy. Shots rang out and two more Australians fell to the ground. One was Able Seaman Robert Moffatt[13] of Sydney. One of the men given the task of carrying him back to the ship, Gus Shea, reported that Seaman Moffatt, in terrible pain, began calling out for his mother. These heart-rending cries had been heard on a battlefield many times before and many times since that fateful September day.

Sadly, AB Moffatt died aboard the *Berrima* the next day and was buried at sea. Able Seaman Daniel Skillen[14] was shot in the elbow. His wound was dressed and he was taken back to the *Yarra*.

To the north and just off the coast HMAS *Encounter* was carrying out its patrol duties, ensuring that no German vessel entered the area unannounced. William Miller did not personally know either Brian Pockley or Charles Elwell. Nor was he aware of what was happening on the road from Kabakaul to Bitapaka.

However the *Encounter* did have a small role to play in the battle already underway. This would come later and in a slightly different location.

13 Signalman R.D.Moffatt; RANR, Engineer of Sydney; b. Lostwithiel, Cornwall, England Dec.1894, Killed in action, 11 Sept.1914.

14 AB Seaman D.S. Skillen; Labourer of Sydney, b. Androssan, Scotland.

Chapter 7

PUSHING ON

"Victory belongs to the most persevering."

(Napoleon Bonaparte)

Lieutenant-Commander Charles Bingham Elwell was now the highest ranking officer among the attacking force on the Bitapaka road. Unaware of that fact, he and his men pushed forward to catch up with Lieutenant Bowen. Having quickly ensured that the German mine, detected almost by accident, was now no longer a threat, they moved on.

Soon Elwell came upon Hill and the wounded Bowen. Elwell realised that most of Hill's men were on the left hand side of the road and so he decided to follow Bowen's advice and move across the road to the right hand side. Gillam ordered some stretcher bearers to pick up Lieutenant Bowen before he moved forward to join Elwell and his men. Elwell took over command from Hill at about 1pm. He directed Hill to continue the advance on the left flank.

All the while bullets continued to thud into the trees around the attackers. Oddly none of Hill's men had been hit; the native troops had been instructed to fire at men in khaki uniforms or those wearing pith helmets (officers). The mufti attire of Hill and his men may well have confused the enemy.

Lieutenant – Commander C.B. Elwell in full dress uniform
(Official History of WWI – C.E.W. Bean)

Across the other side of the road Elwell and his men made good progress and were soon about 80 metres from the enemy trench. At this point Lieutenant-Commander Charles Elwell decided to employ a strategy which was to be repeated on many occasions during the remaining years of World War I. Ordering his men to "Fix Bayonets" he drew his sword from its scabbard and led his now-cheering men forward. A volley of shots rang out. Elwell was shot through the heart and killed instantly. His men dropped and scrambled for cover. Charles Bingham Elwell died two days short of his 31st birthday.

Elwell's action was a brave but also a somewhat foolish one. He had led the first Australian charge on an enemy emplacement on foreign soil during World War I. The enemy fire continued and it was with great difficulty that Petty Officer Sandys retrieved Elwell's body. Elwell was buried near to the spot where he fell; his journey across the world and through Life were both at an end.

Meanwhile, on the left flank Lieutenant Hill, unaware of Elwell's death, continued to advance with his men. Sandys took over the right flank and did the same. Lieutenant Kempf, in charge of the eight Germans and twenty New Guineans defending the trench now saw his position as hopeless as he was outnumbered and outflanked. The relentless advance of the Australians was such that later German reports recounted that by now some native soldiers were cowering at the bottom of the trench. The Germans waved a white flag and Hill replied by waving a nearby seaman's white straw hat.

Lieutenant Kempf did not speak English and so negotiations were conducted through a Sergeant Ritter who spoke English fluently. Some of Hill's party were surprised at how quickly the Germans surrendered but at that stage the Australians had no way of accurately assessing the numerical strength of their enemy. The Germans, on the other hand, knew they were outnumbered.

This was not the only surprise to confront the Australians. Noticing the motley attire of Hill, Kempf refused to surrender to what he perceived as a low-ranking officer. Whilst deciding how to deal with this he was offered a drink of King Edward VII whisky. Hill accepted the offer. In later recalling the incident he would joke that he would have reached the trench more quickly had he known that there was a drink to be had, such was the extent of their thirsts. AB Seaman Sullivan[1] was happy to accept the offer of a drink of mineral water. (1)

Hill was able to negotiate an arrangement with Kempf. It was agreed that the prisoners would be escorted back down the road to Hill's superior, Commander Beresford. Upon arrival a lengthy discussion took place. Finally Kempf agreed to surrender the wireless station and the German forces remaining to defend it. Kempf also agreed to return to the wireless station and explain the new situation to those still in defensive positions. He was to be escorted by No. 6 Company under the command of Lieutenant Bond[2] who had come forward with Commander Beresford.

The ordeal was far from over. The attackers were about to encounter unexpected obstacles placed in their path. They were also to fall foul of German treachery… or at least the treachery of one German officer.

With Captain Harcus[3] in charge, thirty men, a machine gun section and Lieutenant Bond returned to the trench. Also in this

1 AB Seaman T. Sullivan, Labourer of Upper Mitcham, South Australia, b. London, 5 February, 1877.

2 Commr. T.A.Bond; DSO V.D; RANR, Accountant, b. Bishops Waltham, Hants, England,1872.

3 Major J.L. Harcus 20th Btn. AIF, Barrister of Manly, NSW; b. Orkney Islands, Scotland 22 Nov., 1881, Killed in action at Gallipoli, 11 December, 1915.

group was Colonel Holmes' son-in-law, Captain Travers. After a short reluctance the Germans surrendered. They were sent back to the shore under an escort.

The attackers continued to move cautiously down the track. A few shots were fired in their direction but no one was hit. After a further three kilometres they came upon a second German trench. Immediately the three German and twenty native defenders surrendered.

Bond was in the process of disarming the prisoners whilst Captain Travers and the others moved forward. Suddenly shots rang out. Three Australians were hit. Sergeant Ritter, the hospitable German who had previously offered the whisky, had rallied some defenders to attack the Australians. Lieutenant Bond immediately shot Ritter dead. Sergeant Ritter's treachery cost him his life; he was the only German killed during this battle.

Able Seaman Harry Street[4] had been badly wounded from bullets to the back and legs. He died soon afterwards and was buried at the scene. AB Seaman Tim Sullivan was hit by as many as nine bullets. His recovery was a slow and steady process. AB Seaman James Tonks[5] received a bullet wound to the fleshy part of his left calf. This was dressed and he was returned to the *Australia*.

Ritter's treachery had caused considerable consternation among the Australians and their prisoners. Seaman Sullivan recalled the incident in an interview with the *Evening News* after he had returned home:

"There was a general stampede of our prisoners, including the German who had just before offered me the drink. He was instantly shot dead.

4 AB Seaman H.W. Street; Killed in action 11 September, 1914.

5 AB Seaman J.H. Tonks; Labourer, b. Port Adelaide, 14 September,1880, later served in France with the Australian artillery as a Gunner.

"I think I was shot over the eye at the outset, but I kept on, every now and again feeling something hitting me. We got almost to hand to hand fighting and might have used our bayonets to better effect. I brought my rifle to the shoulder for a third shot when my left hand was shattered at such close quarters that I felt the burn more than the pain of the wound.

"That finished me, and I was laid out with two others... Street and Tonks, in the bush, where we had to lie without bandages from 4pm till 11pm. Poor Street was in terrible agony and continually prayed that he might die. The poor fellow's prayer was answered." (2)

The machine gun detachment had thus laboured hard as they carried their equipment down the track. They were left behind to guard the prisoners. Bond, Travers and the German Kempf, continued to move forward. The men could almost sense that they were nearing victory. They also met with a final but determined show of resistance. With them was Conrad Eitel, the Sydney journalist, who had replaced Ritter as interpreter.

Bond's bravery

The advancing party first met a German on a bicycle. After capturing him they learnt that the wireless station had been dismantled and moved to Toma, the new German headquarters. Soon after this they captured another German messenger; this one on horseback. He carried the false message which Bowen had earlier created. Senior German officials were being informed that 800 Australians were advancing on them.

Such news would have buoyed the Australian's spirits. At Kempf's suggestion the horseman was sent on to the wireless station to tell them to surrender as further resistance was useless.

The Australians moved on until, about a kilometre from the wireless station they came upon a party of eight Germans armed with pistols and twenty New Guinean soldiers armed with rifles. To the surprise of the Australians the Germans did not surrender. Instead they began to discuss among themselves just what they should do.

The situation was cleverly defused by Lieutenant Bond. With considerable bravery and great resourcefulness he simply walked up to the Germans and relieved them of their pistols before they could properly react. The New Guinea soldiers were unable to do anything as their officers were standing between them and the Australians.

Captain Travers later recounted the incident and Lieutenant Bond in an interview with war correspondent, F.S. Burnell:

"He strolled along the road as though he were out for a picnic, talking about the various plants we were passing at the side of the road. He's an enthusiastic botanist. There he was, discoursing on Lepidoptera and such, with the imminent risk at every moment of being picked off by some nigger (sic) up a tree. 'Splendid' is the only word I can imagine for his coolness." (3)

It would have been Captain Travers' report to his father-in-law Colonel Holmes that led to Lieutenant Bond being awarded with the Distinguished Service Order. Although not awarded until 11th January, 1916 this was to be the first military decoration awarded to a member of the Australian forces during World War I.

Bond was destined to again have his name in *The London Gazette*. He was twice mentioned in despatches for his further two acts of bravery whilst serving overseas on 11 December, 1915 and 10 April, 1916. (4)

Goal achieved

Escorting the prisoners Travers, Bond and Eitel marched the final kilometre to the wireless station at Toma. They found it deserted as all defenders had fled upon receipt of Kempf's message. Half an hour later Buller arrived with reinforcements. The prisoners were placed under guard: the Germans were housed in the upper storey of the wireless station; the natives in an outside storeroom. Even though the towers for the station had been destroyed by the Germans, the machinery was found to be in working order.

The Australians settled down for the night. It was 7pm.

Chapter 8

THE SIEGE OF TOMA

"The skillful leader subdues the enemy's troops without fighting."

(Sun Tzu)

As the Australians were landed at Kabakaul a force of twenty-five reservists, a member of the medical corps and a telegraphist were landed at Herbertshohe under the command of Sub-Lieutenant Webber[1]. They were accompanied by Lieutenant-Commander, later Captain,[2] Finlayson and a small group from HMAS *Sydney*.

Finlayson carried with him a letter from Rear Admiral Patey addressed to the Acting German Governor Dr. Haber. This letter had been carefully composed by Patey. It called on the Germans to immediately cease any wireless communications and to surrender Rabaul and the German dependencies. Patey was quite prepared to use threats veiled in polite terms:

"I will point out to Your Excellency that the force at my disposal is so large as to render useless any opposition on your part, and such resistance can only result in unnecessary bloodshed.

"Your Excellency will also be good enough to state when you will

1 Sub.-Lt., C.Webber, RANR, Bookkeeper of Melbourne, b. 16 Jan., 1890. Later served with Aust. Artillery in France, gaining the rank of Major.

2 Captain J.F. Finlayson, R.N., of Leichhardt, NSW; b. Sydney, 12 May, 1883.

interview me or my representative with the object of transferring control.

"It is desirable in the interests of yourself and of the inhabitants that this should be arranged as soon as possible.

I have the honour to be, Sir,

Your Excellency's obedient servant,

GEORGE E. PATEY

Rear Admiral Commanding H.M.Australian Fleet." (1)

Finlayson was unable to locate Dr. Haber (who was in Toma). He handed the letter to a German civilian who promised to get it to Haber. While Finlayson and his men remained in Herbertshohe to guard their stores, Sub-Lieutenant Webber and the reservists set off for Toma. After travelling about halfway without meeting any opposition they decided to return as dark was fast approaching.

At 6pm Rear Admiral Patey received a reply from Dr. Haber. The reply would not have pleased Patey. In an effort to play for time Haber, declined to surrender on the grounds that he was only acting Governor and therefore did not have the proper authority. Haber also refused to stop wireless communication. He was hoping that the German fleet would return to the area. In fact the *Melbourne* and the *Warrego* had just been sent to New Ireland as the result of a baseless rumour which said the German ships *Geier* and *Prinz Eitel Friedrich* were there. Haber also claimed that Patey should not have begun negotiations whilst fighting was going on.

Rear Admiral Patey was not ready to quibble. He replied that hostilities had begun because Haber had taken eleven hours to reply when he was only ten miles (sixteen kilometres) away. He also implied that future communications should be addressed to Colonel Holmes.

Patey was anxious to return to Sydney to pursue other duties. Under a previous arrangement he was about to leave for Sydney with the light cruisers returning to be refitted for convoy duties. Haber was also told to direct his reply to Colonel Holmes who had been charged with the task of taking over the administration of the colony. Formal control of the operation was handed to Colonel Holmes on 12th September. Holmes' first action was to send HMAS *Berrima* to Rabaul where four infantry companies quickly took control, hauling down all enemy flags. That same day Holmes sent a demand to Dr. Haber again calling on him to surrender. This time Haber replied that he would make his response known at 4.30pm the next day (13 September).

At 3pm on Sunday 13th September Colonel Holmes formally proclaimed the occupation of German possessions in New Guinea by hoisting the flag in Rabaul. Historians do not seem to agree as to which flag was hoisted. According to S.S. MacKenzie it was the British flag (2) but A.W. Jose, also an official historian writing under the guidance of C.E.W. Bean, stated that the Australian flag was raised (3). The war correspondent, F.S. Burnell put together a pictorial account. He too claimed the British flag was raised but his photo of the Proclamation ceremony does not show the flag itself (4).

The original British instructions to Australia regarding this campaign had clearly stated that any territory occupied was to be at the disposal of the British government. In light of this, it was the Union Jack which now flew at Rabaul.

Later that same afternoon Holmes received Dr. Haber's reply. Again Haber claimed he had no authority to surrender. Holmes was in no mood to accept this reply. He conferred with Admiral Patey and then decided to send men to arrest Haber.

Proclamation of British Occupation
AWM: P03078 007

HMAS *Encounter's* Field Gun Crew
AWM: 300634

At 5 o'clock on the morning of 14th September Colonel Watson set out for Toma with four companies of infantry, a machine gun crew and one twelve-pounder gun from HMAS *Encounter*. They left at dawn and as they marched the 6-inch guns of the *Encounter* began to shell an outlying ridge near Toma. This was the first shot "fired in anger" by the Royal Australian Navy.

William Miller was already awake when this shelling began. In fact he had been about his duties for some time as everyone on board was well aware that some exciting developments were about to take place. In the years to come he seldom spoke of his experiences during the Great War, except for this particular incident. William frequently told his mates whilst having a beer… "I was aboard the *Encounter* when we shelled the Germans…"

Meanwhile Colonel Watson and his men met no opposition. Aside from a few native police they met no one in uniform. As they got closer to Toma, Watson decided to reinforce the earlier message from the *Encounter*. The 12-pounder was set up and used to send off a few shells. According to one witness this was done to "impress a few locals" and impress them they did. Anyone with plans to resist immediately dropped those plans. The Australians set about searching the surrounding buildings for stores and weapons. Some rifles, pistols, uniforms and even a jewelled sword were found. There was one particularly curious incident when they entered one house and found a woman lying on a bed, apparently ill.

"To make sure the bed was searched also, with the result that the mattress was found to be stuffed with rifles. The lady's convalescence is not thought to have suffered any serious retardation by her disturbance." (5)

Haber now had no choice but to respond. Dr. Haber agreed to present himself to Colonel Holmes at Herbertshohe the next day. He did so at 11am on 15th September. Whilst he and Holmes discussed terms a French cruiser (*Montcalm*) passed by, clearly indicating to Haber, the unity of purpose and resolve which he now faced. Negotiations continued all afternoon. Finally it was agreed to make a final settlement at Herbertshohe at noon on 17th September.

Haber was to suffer a further short bout of anxiety. Contrary winds that day delayed Holmes' arrival and he began to fear that negotiations were at an end. Finally when Holmes did arrive a further two hours of talks took place before the Terms of Capitulation were formally signed. Holmes' signature was witnessed by Commander Stevenson of HMAS *Encounter* whilst Captain von Klewitz witnessed that of Dr. Haber.

Terms of Capitulation

As government documents go, the Terms of Capitulation, dated 17th September, 1914, were quite straightforward. However, some of them were to cause considerable controversy.

"(1)The name Deutsch Neu Guinea (German New Guinea) includes the whole of the German Possessions in the Pacific Ocean lately administered from Rabaul by the said Acting Governor on behalf of the German Imperial Government, and the said Possessions are hereafter referred to as 'The Colony'." (6)

The term, German New Guinea, covered all German possessions in the Pacific Islands with the exception of Samoa. It therefore included the Marshalls and the Carolines as well as the Bismarck Archipelago.

Some were later to claim that the Marshalls and the Carolines, which were later handed over to Japan, had really been surrendered to Australia. However this is not the case: Haber had deliberately refused to surrender territory. He had simply guaranteed non-resistance of any German forces occupying the islands.

"All military resistance to the said military occupation of the Colony shall cease forthwith." (7)

Officers of the German Regular Forces were to be regarded as prisoners of war. However all other officers and non-commissioned men (reservists) were to be allowed to return to their homes and their normal occupations after taking an oath of neutrality. German administrative officials were also to be allowed to remain in their present positions providing they too took an oath of neutrality.

These provisions were later to be a cause of some concern as a result of how they performed their duties and also because of the response of one particular German soldier to the German surrender.

Under Point 8 (of a total of twelve clauses) "all monies and properties…are to be handed over to the said Colonel Holmes, Brigadier Commanding". (8)

In view of the earlier measures taken by the Germans regarding their Treasury monies this provision was also to become a cause of concern for Colonel Holmes.

Dr. Haber gave an undertaking that he would take no further part, directly or indirectly in the war. As a result, he was to be allowed to return to Germany to advise the government of the terms of surrender.

When news of the Terms of Capitulation reached Australia the public reaction was less than favourable. As stories came back of German atrocities, real and imagined, committed in Europe, there developed in Australia an intense groundswell of anti-German sentiment. Added to this was the long-term view that New Guinea was an area of special concern to Australia. Many wondered why the Germans were not simply ejected and their possessions seized. In a dispatch of 26th December, 1914 Holmes felt it necessary to defend his actions. He pointed out that his task had been to seize the wireless stations and to set up a temporary administration; his role did not involve proclaiming formal annexation. (9)

As agreed under the terms of capitulation those German troops still outside Herbertshohe marched from Toma on the morning of 21st September and at 10 o'clock lay down their arms. That is all... except one man... his story was to emerge much later.

Dr. Haber, Capt. Von Klewitz arrive prior to surrender.
AWM: H12842

Mopping up: Part 1... Follow the money

On the day the Terms of Capitulation were signed (17th September), a force of seventy men were sent from Herbertshohe to recover the German Treasury funds. Led by Lieutenants V.H.B. Sampson[3] and I.B. Sherbon[4] these men were to encounter severe difficulties over the next nine days. The Australians were well aware that they may meet up with some Germans who either did not know about, or did not agree to, the surrender. In addition they were entering rugged terrain with dense vegetation.

To make their task even more complicated the treasure had been placed in three locations known as Places "A", "B" and "C". Upon reaching Toma they were met by a force of 26 Germans and 79 natives who, fortunately agreed to surrender. Here the first portion of the treasure was handed over.

After resting for an hour the Australians moved a further five miles (eight kilometres) down a narrow track to Place B where the Germans had their field wireless station. At this stage they did not locate the booty. The next day Sampson, Sherbon and seven men moved on to Place C where they found Dr. Haber in camp with ten cases of gold and notes and some silver. He received them in a friendly manner and handed over the funds.

Dr. Haber re-directed the Australians to Place B where, rather ironically, the treasure was found buried under one of the tents used by some of the men the night before. All of the treasure was sealed up

3 Maj. V.H.B.Sampson, of Sydney, NSW, b. Upper Manilla, Killed in action, Fromelles, 9 July, 1916.

4 Maj. I.B.Sherbon, of La Perouse, NSW; b. Forest Lodge, NSW, Killed in action, Flers, 14 November, 1916.

and along with the wireless plant, placed on wagons found at Place A for the return journey to Herbertshohe.

The treasury funds had been recovered without encountering hostile resistance. There was however a sad outcome for the two leaders of this expedition. Both Sampson and Sherbon later enlisted in the AIF and both were killed on the Western Front; the former at Fromelles (19th July, 1916) and the latter at Flers (14th November, 1916). (10)

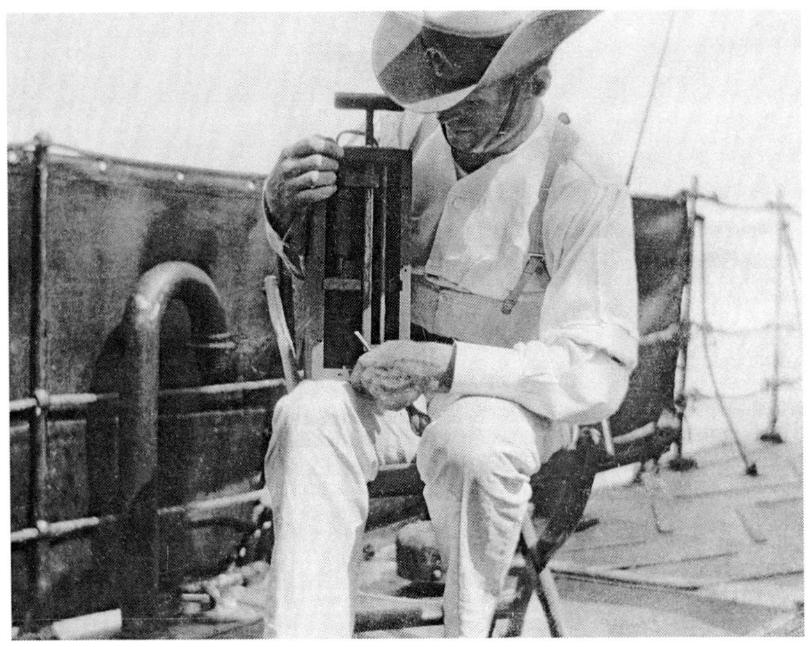

Gunner Yeo with the key of a landmine.
AWM: J03325

Mopping up Part 2…Finishing with a bang

There still remained the problem of the mines which the Germans had placed on the road from Kabakaul to Bitapaka. As stated earlier the first mine had been discovered when an Australian seaman was attacked by a native who tried to relieve him of his rifle. The native was shot as he ran away. Upon investigating the incident, Signal-Boatswain Hunter had found the mine and disconnected the firing key.

Apparently, fortune had been kind to the Australians with respect to the second set of explosives. Major Molloy asked the German officer, Lieutenant Mayer, why the mines had not been set off. He was told that one of the wireless operators at Bitapaka had been put in charge of the mines but a day or so before the Australians had landed, the wireless operator had fallen ill with malaria and died. No one had been delegated to take over his role and so the mines were not detonated, allowing the Australians to pass by unharmed.

On 4th January, 1915 a team was sent to inspect the area where the mine had been found. They dug up a seven metre long tube filled with dynamite. This was detonated where it lay, resulting in a huge crater. The hole measured some 27 feet long, 15 feet in depth and seven feet deep. The next day, whilst filling in this hole, another set of wires was found leading to another tube also loaded with dynamite. This time the explosives were taken into the bush and detonated so as to avoid damaging the road. (11)

No one was injured when the two mines were detonated four months after the original landing.

Removing a landmine, January 1915
AWM: P02031 002 2

Chapter 9

THE ROLE OF THE ROYAL AUSTRALIAN NAVY

"Endeavour."

(motto of HMAS *Australia* (1), RAN's first flagship).

There is little doubt that the success of the AN&MEF in achieving its objective, control over the German colonies of New Guinea, was largely due to the role played by the Royal Australian Navy. This fledgling body acquitted itself extremely well. It certainly justified the decisions made by the Australian government to create a naval force native to Australia in the years just prior to the war.

The RAN was seen as a separate and complete unit in its own waters even if it was doing the bidding of the British government. Its success could not have occurred without the assistance of that government in building the Australian fleet. The German East Asiatic Squadron was a formidable force with its armoured cruisers *Scharnhorst* and *Gneisenau* and their highly trained crews. On the other hand the *Sydney* and *Melbourne* were modern. So too were the three destroyers and the two submarines; the *Encounter* was old but serviceable.

The decision to retain the battle-cruiser *Australia* as the Australian flagship rather than attach it to the Royal Navy in European waters was a significant one. It is generally accepted that without HMAS *Australia* the RAN would have been totally outclassed by the German squadron. During the period soon after the German surrender, the German East Asiatic Squadron chose to head toward South American waters. This decision was no doubt due to a combination of "discretion being the better part of valour" and the fact that they were more urgently needed elsewhere. It was also a decision which led to the Japanese Navy becoming more actively involved in areas south of the China seas.

The only reason that Australia could seriously contemplate dispatching a force to assume control of German colonial possessions in New Guinea was the fact that it had a serviceable fleet. Whilst the total naval personnel operating this fleet may have been few in number they were not necessarily inexperienced. At the outbreak of war in 1914, the RAN had a total of 3800 personnel of which 850 (22%) had a Royal Navy background. (1)There were a total of sixteen RAN vessels, including the two submarines, *AE1* and *AE2*. (2)

It is hard for a current day reader to imagine the sense of trepidation that would have been experienced by those British seamen now serving with a very young naval force far-removed from their homeland. Their journey to Australian waters may well have been a difficult one and contact with their families intermittent. It has been said that some among them were trying to escape their family responsibilities; others were acting out of a sense of adventure. It was this same sense of adventure which later motivated many of the men in both the AN&MEF and the AIF to travel across the seas to face the German foe. A significant number of those British seaman later chose to make Australia their home.

It is also true that the Australian government's decision to introduce a system of military training for citizen forces proved to be a wise decision. It led to the emergence of capable officers who proved efficient and adaptable enough to lead an expeditionary force. Lieutenant Bowen was one such officer. These men were operating with others who had been extremely well trained by the Royal Navy, for example Lieutenant-Commander Besant and Lieutenant-Commander Elwell. A number of these officers were later to be rewarded with the, no longer current, military decoration, V.D. designating "Volunteer Officers' Decoration".

Overall the role of the RAN was to oversee the conveyance of the men of the AN&MEF and their supplies to the New Guinea area and to act as their guardian angels. In reality, looking back on the tasks actually performed, they were involved in a variety of roles.

The RAN:

- conducted attacks of its own e.g. shelling Toma.
- took control of a number of small German vessels
- conveyed men to the various outposts after the Capitulation.
- conducted searches for missing vessels, notably the *AE1*.

Their task of conveying men and supplies to designated destinations was carried out efficiently. Once the Australians had secured German possessions in New Guinea and the immediate area, Colonel Holmes was keen to move on to the outposts, both nearby and further afield, north of the equator, to places such as Yap. It had been one of his targets as set by the British government when the AN&MEF was first formed. This view was not shared by Admiral Patey who saw pursuit of the German fleet as his prime concern. Essentially the different perceptions were due to the fact that although this expedition was a military and naval joint-task each of the two leaders viewed it from a different perspective. There was no open disagreement between them but circumstances, as will be seen, had changed, and Holmes was as yet unaware of the bigger picture.

First in…

The first action in this campaign actually occurred just one month prior to the landing at Herbertshohe. On 12th August 1914, under the supervision of HMAS *Sydney,* Australian destroyers entered Blanche Bay on a reconnaissance mission. Landing parties went ashore seeking information on the wireless station. Unsuccessful in gaining this information they resorted to destroying the telephones at the Herbertshohe and Rabaul post offices.

Those German civilians encountered during this escapade were no doubt lying to the Australians when they said they did not know the whereabouts of the wireless station. On the other hand they would also have been rather apprehensive as to what was yet to come. The arrival of the Australians, whilst not unexpected, was not a pleasant experience for them.

On the same day HMS *Hampshire* put the wireless station at Yap in the Caroline Islands out of action. For a short period the Germans were still able to relay war news from Samoa through Nauru. This situation ended on 9th September when a landing party from HMAS *Melbourne* put ashore at Nauru and wrecked the wireless installation there.

The German Protectorate, the areas in and around New Guinea, was now isolated. Hostilities on the Bitapaka Road began two days later. HMAS *Encounter* shelled the ridge near Toma on 14th September, 1914. With one exception those two dates encapsulate the period when shots were fired in anger during this campaign.

Officers and crew of HMAS '*Encounter*', circa 1913/14
Courtesy of Miller and Ellis families.

Acquisition of German vessels

During the time of land-based hostilities near Rabaul, the RAN captured a number of smaller German craft. Aside from the *Komet* and the *Siar* none of them were of great significance. As mentioned in an earlier chapter, the first prize claimed by the RAN was the former British steamer *Zambezi* which had been commandeered by the Germans to carry supplies for the Rabaul wireless station from their base at Nauru. It was claimed by the crew of HMAS *Encounter* about a week after war had been declared and almost a month before hostilities began at Bitapaka.

Date	**Ship's Name and Tons (t)**	**Details about Capture**
11 Sept 1914	*Sumatra* 584 t	Cape Tawaii
13 Sept 1914	*Madang* 194 t	By *Protector*, Herbertshohe
14 Sept 1914	*Nusa* 60 t	By *Warrego*, Kawieng
18 Sept 1914	*Siar* 450 t *Matupi*, *Senta*	By *Nusa*-Gardner Islands, New Ireland. *Matupi* and *Senta* were motor-schooners belonging to the *Siar*.
23 Sept 1914	*Meklong* 438 t *Brass Monkey*	By *Parramatta*, Duke of York Island Motor launch, tender for *Brass Monkey*
11 Oct 1914	*Komet*	By *Nusa*, New Britain
26 Oct 1914	*Samoa*	By *Madang*, New Britain

The *SIAR* was owned by the New German Company. The ship's original purpose had been to carry provisions for the company. Once war had been declared she began to supply coal to the *Komet*. In early October she delivered supplies to the Admiralty group and then headed towards New Ireland.

It is at this stage that she became too daring. Holmes grew suspicious when the German settlers there grew less keen to buy Australian provisions. He suspected that smuggling was involved. As a result he despatched the *Nusa* to Kawieng to take control. It was then that the Australians learnt that the *Siar* could be found lurking in the nearby Gardner group of islands. The military force attached to the *Nusa* were quickly sent in pursuit. (3)

This pursuit took place directly after the occupation of Kawieng, the administrative centre of New Ireland. Led by Major Heritage and piloted by a civilian, John Strasburg, the *Nusa* left at night and the next day entered Tikitere Harbour (Tabar Island) under the cover of a thick haze. They found the *Siar* and its two motor schooners at anchor with all officers ashore, breakfasting.

Before the Germans could react they were quickly disarmed and the ship's papers were seized. The prize vessel, the *Siar*, was towed back to Kawieng having had its motors disabled. Colonel Holmes was extremely pleased with the outcome. In his report he was glowing in his discussion of Strasburg's role. He also made special mention of the services of Petty Officer Clarke[1], who took charge of the *Siar*, and AB Seaman Courtman[2] who worked on getting its engines into working order.(4)

1 Petty Officer G.I. Clarke, b. Sussex, England, 6 Jan., 1870.

2 AB Seaman C.C. Courtman of Sydney, b. Essex, England, 1871. Later appointed Warrant Officer in the infantry of the AN&MEF.

The *KOMET* was a yacht used by the German administration. It was listed in their administrative papers as such and Colonel Holmes had fully expected that it would have been surrendered at the time of the capitulation. However when war broke out the *Komet* was handed over to German naval authorities. To all intents and purposes the *Komet* became a warship. The capture of this vessel meant that German log books and wireless diaries fell into Australian possession. These proved quite valuable.

Capturing the *Komet* was no easy task. It remained at large, generally in the New Britain area until 11 October, 1914. At times her crew were out of radio contact with their countrymen but they did learn of Rabaul's capitulation. The Australians at Rabaul were keen to snare the *Komet* as they were wary of its ability to provide intelligence to larger German warships.

As HMAS *Encounter* was on its way to Suva, Holmes commissioned Commander Jackson[3] to man the (recently-captured) *Nusa* with men from the Naval brigade, arm her and go in search of the *Komet*. Acting on information provided by friendly natives, the *Nusa* was able to catch the *Komet* unawares near a peninsula on the north coast of New Britain.

Commander Jackson and his crew acquitted themselves admirably. Before dawn they ran in through some reefs at half-speed, steaming to within fifty yards of the *Komet*. Colonel Paton[4] led the boarding party and discovered the German Captain, Moller, shaving in his cabin. (5)

---

3 Commander J.M. Jackson, R.N., Commanded HMAS *Una* 1914/16.

4 Maj.-Gen. J. Paton C.B. CMG V.D., Commanded 7th Inf. Bde., AIF 1915/17;6th Inf. Bde. AIF 1917/18, Merchant of Newcastle, b.18 Nov., 1867.

The *Komet* was taken to Sydney where it was converted into an Australian warship and commissioned as HMAS *Una* on 17th November, 1914. The name, *Una*, was chosen as it was thought that it meant, "first " (as in the first warship captured by the RAN). It actually means "the only one" and so it was; the only warship captured in New Guinea waters by the RAN. (6)

Occupation of German Outposts

The delivery of men and equipment to designated destinations was carried out efficiently. This duty began on 14 August 1914 with the departure of the AN&MEF from Sydney bound for New Guinea. Including a brief interlude for training at Palm Island, this phase of the operation was completed by 9 September. All was then made ready for the assault on Rabaul.

When land-based hostilities concluded, the RAN, using its own vessels or those it had commandeered, was involved in the occupation of the various outposts. These operations took place between late September and early December, 1914. In chronological order these were:

22-24 September 1914 Occupation of Madang – This was the most important German administrative centre apart from Rabaul. Australian Naval vessels *Australia, Berrima* and *Encounter* were accompanied by the French naval ship *Montcalm.* The Germans offered no resistance but they were guilty of some devious behaviour…

William Miller remained onboard HMAS *Encounter* after the shelling of Toma but his duties changed slightly. A spirit of jubilation had begun to circulate amongst all those in the AN&MEF and it was not long before this also touched those serving on their "guardian angels", the Australian Naval vessels, especially the *Encounter*. Excited discussions about their recent involvement were common. When he wasn't busy tending to the celebrations of the officers, William Miller joined his shipmates in their celebrations. They were well aware that the firing of *Encounter's* guns had successfully led to the final German capitulation but they were not yet aware of the place those shots had in Australian naval history. Amid much back-slapping a common comment was…

"When the guns went off I thought the sky had fallen in. I bet the Germans couldn't get undercover quick enough…"

The *Encounter*, carrying a white flag, was sent to the harbour entrance. William Miller, was later to tell his children:

"Some of us were quite concerned. We had no way of knowing if the enemy were lying in wait with weapons ready to fire or…worse still…with mines waiting for us in the water. We were hoping that all would be well as we felt that all opposition had ceased…particularly after we fired off our guns at them a few days earlier."

A launch was sent ashore. On board were Captain Travers, Lieutenant Jens Lyng[5] as interpreter and the captured German, Lieutenant Mayer. They met no opposition but once again they were to learn about German subterfuge. The Australians came upon the deputy District Officer who told them that the District Officer had left day two days early on an expedition to punish some rebellious natives.

This was a lie. He had actually fled to Port Alexis, twenty kilometres north of Madang. From there he went to Yap, in the Caroline Islands where he was later captured and interned. Captain Travers escorted his deputy, one other official and a German civilian back to HMAS *Australia*

5 Capt. Jens Lyng, Draftsman and Linguist in Commonwealth Bureau of Census and Statistics 1920-32, Librarian 1929-32, of Caulfield, Vic., b.Hasle, Denmark 16 April, 1868.

where they agreed to surrender, assured the Australians there were no mines in the harbour and that there would be no German resistance.

As the Australian warships trained their guns on the town, the chief citizen raised the white flag. The ships steamed through the heads to a position from which they landed a party of 12 men. The German flag was quickly hauled down and the Union Jack hoisted in its place. The remainder of that day was spent confiscating all arms and obliging the Germans to take the oath of neutrality. After a long day the Australians went to bed and slept well.

Major Edward Martin[6] was placed in charge of the Australian garrison at Madang. He was to be supported by a half-company of Naval reserves, a company and a half of infantry and a medical corps detachment. Holmes and the rest of the group returned to Rabaul at 6pm that same day.

There was a minor disturbance the next day. A group of native police tried to desert their post. Shots were fired over their heads. As they ran away further shots were fired and several natives dropped their backpacks. Six sticks of dynamite were found among them.

More disturbing were the plans adopted by the Germans but later, thankfully, abandoned. A German official had fled to Port Alexis where he had met up with the District Officer. Also at the port was the German ship the *Kormoran*. Plans were made to take her to Yap, pick up the garrison there and return to make a surprise attack on Madang. Most of the garrison actually boarded the *Kormoran* on the night of 29th September. However the plan came to nought. It is believed that the District Officer had pointed out that there would be adverse consequences for those Germans still in Madang. (7)

---

6 Brig.-Gen. E.F. Martin, C.B., CMG, DSO, V.D., Commanded 5th Inf.Bde.AIF 1918-19, Accountant of Waverley, NSW, b.Launceston, Tas., 22 Aug. 1875.

16-17 October 1914 Occupation of Kawieng – Kawieng was the main German administrative centre on New Ireland. For Holmes there were two specific issues to be dealt with aside from formally claiming the area.

When the Germans moved their headquarters out of the Rabaul area they had interned Jolley, the British consul, on New Ireland. He was also a plantation owner and had refused to sign an agreement with the Germans that he would make no effort to contact the Australian warships unless they allowed him to remain on his property. This they refused to allow. Holmes wanted to free Jolley and to capture the *Siar*.

To this end, Colonel Holmes despatched Major Heritage in charge of fifteen men and a machine gun onboard the *Nusa*. Accompanying them was civilian, John Strasburg, an experienced operator of island schooners, acting as navigator. Upon arrival at Kawieng Heritage found that Jolley was on a plantation some twenty miles away. In quick succession he secured Jolley's release and the surrender of the German District Officer. He then turned his attention to the recovery of the *Siar*.

5-6 November 1914 Occupation of Nauru – Nauru was of particular significance as it had been, until 9 September, a significant part of the German communications network. Its only commercial value was phosphate for use as a fertiliser. Colonel Holmes led this expedition himself. He was accompanied by Captain Norrie[7] and Lieutenant Fisher[8] onboard SS *Messina*.

Special problems arose during this expedition. On an earlier visit by HMAS *Melbourne* German officials had given their word not to

7 Brigadier .E.C. Norrie, C.B., DSO V.D., Commanded 28th Btn. AIF, b.Grafton 28 September, 1885.

8 Lieut. A.D. Fisher, Solicitor of Sydney, b. North Sydney 14 December, 1882.

offer any resistance. They kept their word but there was considerable ill feeling from within the German business community. After a hurried visit by HMAS *Melbourne* two days before the assault at Bitapaka when the wireless station had been put out of action, the German residents had burnt a red British ensign and had erected a tombstone to "the departed British".

The landing at Nauru was a problem in itself. Due to the conditions of the surf it was difficult and slow, accomplished only by surf-boats manned by native crews.

Upon landing on 6th November, Holmes hauled down the German flag and, in an effort to impress loyalty upon the natives, had held a public ceremony during which the British flag was raised and saluted. Holmes realised that the natives may have misunderstood the earlier situation when the *Melbourne* had sailed away. He called together all the native chiefs to tell them that soldiers would remain behind to protect them, that the rule by Germany was over and that as long as they did what was right there would be no problems for them. The point which he most wanted to impart was the fact their arrival and assumption of control was permanent.

When examination was made of the wireless station it was found that it had not been further damaged by the Germans, suggesting to Holmes that they did not expect the British to occupy Nauru and may have intended returning there. Holmes could see its potential for the British and left Nauru having resolved to have qualified men sent there to effect repairs. (8)

19 November 1914 Occupation of the Admiralty group and Western Islands – Major Heritage was again in charge but this time he was onboard the former German vessel, *Siar.* As they approached the island:

"The Germans and native troops were observed through glasses to be armed and retreating in military formation into the interior..."

Heritage may have considered this strange behaviour given that by now news of the capitulation, but more tellingly the shelling of Toma, would have reached the Germans on these islands. Whether or not it had, is essentially irrelevant. Major Heritage was full of resolve and in no mood for procrastination...

"...the *Siar* fired a belt from a maxim over their heads at long range and the Germans capitulated... "

The results were instantaneous. The Germans surrendered without further delay... Major Heritage concluded his report with the opinion...

"I think this is of interest as it was the last hostile firing during the campaign." (9)

This was indeed the last occasion during the whole occupation campaign when shots were actually fired at an armed enemy by the men of the AN&MEF.

Sub-Lieutenant Hext[9] and a garrison of twelve naval ratings were placed in charge at Lorengau, the seat of administration. (10)

9 December 1914 Occupation of the German Solomon Islands – The focus here was on Bougainville. Complications arose due to a change in the priorities of the Department of Defence. Holmes had been

9 Sub-Lt., A.B. Hext, Engineer of Melbourne, b. Ipswich, Qld., 27 July 1890. Served as a Captain with 30th Btn. AIF, Killed in France, 20 June, 1918.

told that he could expect considerable opposition on Bougainville. He was to employ *Una* (formerly the German ship, *Komet*) and await the arrival of HMAT *Eastern* from Sydney. So potentially dangerous was the situation considered, that Holmes was also told that the three Australian destroyers would assist him in occupying German territory south of the equator and also go on to seek German cruisers.

On 7th December these vessels had still not arrived at Rabaul and Holmes learnt that they had been diverted to Madang. Not wanting to further delay proceedings Holmes immediately despatched the *Meklong* with a force of two companies of infantry and a machine-gun section under the command of Lieutenant-Colonel Watson.

Watson and his men successfully took control at Kieta on Bougainville Island. A Proclamation of Occupation was read; the German officials were taken onboard the *Meklong* as prisoners. All other German residents were made to take an oath of neutrality. Lieutenant Maughan[10] was left in charge of the garrison at Bougainville.

Despite misgivings, the occupation of Bougainville had gone ahead peacefully. However this does not mean to say that there had not been a show of defiance from the Germans. The Australians had expected to find at Kieta an administrative steamer of 60 tons by the name of *Buka*. She was a sister ship to the *Nusa*.

This vessel was nowhere to be found. About three weeks before the arrival of the Australian force the *Buka* had been taken into a neighbouring bay and deliberately scuttled. For a time Holmes considered raising the vessel as he considered it could be of use. He even sent down divers from the Una early in 1915 but these plans were themselves scuttled. (11)

10 Lieut-Col. J.M. Maughan, DSO, Solicitor, Edgecliffe, NSW, b. Ashfield 18 Dec. 1877. Commanded 20th Btn. AIF, (temporarily) 1917.

Searching for Missing Vessels

The RAN was involved in two major searches for vessels which went missing in the waters around Rabaul during World War I. Both of these searches involved HMAS *Encounter*, both of them attracted a great deal of interest and concern back in Australia but they were a number of years apart and the outcomes were vastly different. These stories deserve special mention…

Chapter 10

TRAGEDY AMIDST VICTORY

"No one can safely say that he will still be living tomorrow."

(Euripedes)

Amidst the euphoria of the victory over the Germans there arose a tragedy which was to cast a gloom over the men of the AN&MEF and the RAN. At 7am on the 14th September HMAS *Parramatta* set out from Herbertshohe. She was accompanied by the Australian submarine *AE1* which set out from Rabaul. Their appointed task was to search St. George's channel between New Britain and the Duke of York Islands for any sign of German warships.

On this particular day there was a considerable amount of heat haze and so the two vessels occasionally lost sight of each other. They were still in contact with each other at 2:30pm. The *AE1* was last seen at about 3:30pm, south-west of the Duke of York Island, apparently heading back into harbour.

HMAS *Parramatta* returned to Herbertshohe not yet suspecting that something was amiss. When the *AE1* had not returned by 8pm a search was immediately commenced by the *Parramatta* and the *Yarra,*

RAN Submarine *AEI* (taken from HMAS '*Encounter*').
AWM: A02604.1

joined by the *Encounter* and the *Warrego* the next day. In addition motor and steam launches were commandeered from Rabaul and Herbertshohe to help with the search.

Despite an extensive search over an area of some thirty miles (48 kilometres) no sign was ever seen of the missing submarine; not even a tell-tale oil slick was found. The loss of Lieutenant-Commander Besant[1], two officers and thirty two men was deeply felt by those involved in the search. It was Australia's first major loss of World War I.

Numerous theories were put forward as to what may have become of the vessel. Those on board the *Parramatta* were convinced that she had not met up with any vessel, German or otherwise, which may have caused her to dive suddenly. One theory put forward was that the *AE1*

1 Lieutenant-Commr. T.F.Besant, R.N., b.Liverpool, England, 22 Dec.1883, Lost in Submarine, *AE1*, 14 Sept.1914.

may have made a practice dive as it neared Blanche Bay and hit some of the sharp and often overhanging coral in that area. Official historian A.W. Jose regarded this as somewhat unlikely as no traces of oil were found in the area. (1)

Another, more sinister theory, was that the *AE1* was the victim of a hit from a German vessel, the *Kolonialgesellschaft*. This followed a claim made by a captured German believed to be the Captain, Wilhelm August Ewald Reuschel.

Over the years since World War I a number of searches have been made for the vessel. The first serious one was made by RAN Commander John Foster. He was amazed that the RAN files on the *AE1* had barely been opened since 1919. In 1976 he convinced the Navy to allow him to conduct a sonar search from HMAS *Flinders*. A possible contact was made but it was not possible to investigate it.

In 1990 the famous underwater explorer Jacques Cousteau conducted another search. Once again a possible contact was made but could not be investigated due to faulty equipment. In 2007 HMAS *Benalla* with Foster onboard made a sonar identification of a man-made object at an undisclosed location which they believe is the resting place of the submarine. (2).

All of these investigations have stimulated interest from some of the descendants of the crew, many of whom wish the vessel to remain undisturbed. One group recently handed a lengthy report to the Australian government. Led by Dr. Michael White, QC, and with a search committee headed by retired Commodore Terence Roach, this group hopes to conduct a search in time for the centenary of the outbreak of World War I. They believe such a task would need two to three weeks and would cost in excess of $6 million.

At the same time former salvage diver and author, Fritz Herscheid and salvager Brett Devine have joined forces also with the hope of mounting a search. They were acting on information provided during a conversation in 1968 with the last surviving World War I priest who had lived in New Britain. (3)

Thirty-five men lost their lives when the *AE1* went missing; sixteen of them were members of the Royal Australian Navy (see Appendix for *AE1* Honour roll)…

William Miller was onboard HMAS *Encounter* during the original search. For him this was a new and unwanted experience in a number of different ways. Most of their training had been spent on learning naval discipline and how to work smoothly as a team when going into battle. Considerably less time had been spent on search operations and in particular those for vessels believed to have been captured or sunk. He and his shipmates were overcome by a deep sense of concern and, as reality dawned, grief. He did not personally know more than a couple of the crew of the AE1 but that was irrelevant. They had all been working on the same tasks, they had all endured the same problems of adjustment to environmental and operational conditions. William Miller's feelings were those of empathy with as well as sympathy for the crew of the *AE1*.

The loss of the *AE1* and its crew also caused William to re-consider his own future. He had signed up for a three-year term which was not due to end in March, 1916. He began to wonder…" do I really want to be out here at sea, far from home and in a situation where my fate is not entirely in my own hands?"

His reasoning was not that cowardice or of wanting to shirk his duty (as he was to later demonstrate) but more a feeling of helplessness.

When on a ship at sea you may be able to run but you cannot hide. At least on land, or so he reasoned, you can do something to duck down and take cover.

In reality the decision of what was to become of him between the time when the *Encounter* helped search for the *AE1* (September, 1914) and when his period of service ended, was not his to make…

A Naval conundrum: the *Matunga/Wolf* incident

HMAS *Encounter* was again involved in a search for a missing vessel some three years after it had unsuccessfully tried to find the *AE1*. On this occasion the mystery was ultimately solved; the outcome was a cause for celebration, not grief. Nor was William Miller onboard. His life had taken an entirely different path since the time when his period of service in the RAN had ended.

In July 1917 a steamer, owned by the Burns Philp company, left Sydney bound for Rabaul. As well as coal intended for HMAS *Una* it had onboard sixteen men of the expeditionary force, most of them returning from leave. Among these men were four officers all bound for important administrative positions in New Guinea. One of them was Colonel Strangman, a close friend of Colonel Pethebridge[2], the New Guinea Administrator who had replaced Colonel Holmes.

Naval authorities believed the Pacific was free of enemy raiders. An uncoded message was sent to Rabaul informing them of the *Matunga's* departure. On 5th August, 1917 the *Matunga* sent a "clear"

2 Brigadier-General Sir Samuel A. Pethebridge, b. 3 August,1862, d. 25 January, 1918.

message to Rabaul stating its expectation of arrival on 7th August. No further radio messages were received.

Concern began to mount rapidly when the *Matunga* failed to arrive. All sorts of theories were put forward to explain this failure. These ranged from storms, to adverse currents, to broken propeller shafts and to boiler explosions. It was even suggested that an underwater seismic explosion may have claimed the vessel.

HMAS *Una* was sent out to look for the *Matunga*. HMAS *Encounter* was summoned from Sydney and also joined the search. This search went on for several months and in that time it was joined by a large number of vessels — *SS Meklong, SS Marinda, SS Siar, SS Madang* and the mission schooner *Raphael.*

Positive news filtered back to Rabaul in early December. Natives on an island to the north of New Guinea reported finding a bottle in the sea containing a message from prisoners on a German raider. In mid-January the relatives of those missing were told that the men had been captured and most probably were still alive. Late in February of 1918 Germany cockily reported that the auxiliary cruiser *Wolf* had returned home carrying some 400 crew members from a number of vessels including the *Matunga.*

The story of what happened to those men of the AN&MEF onboard the *Matunga* is an interesting one in itself. Soon after the prisoners were taken onto the *Wolf* the Germans sank the *Matunga*. None of the prisoners were to set foot on solid ground for the next seven months as the *Wolf* made a circuitous voyage back to Germany. The prisoners were transferred to a captured Japanese vessel, the *Hitachi Maru*, for the trip to Germany. Most of the men remained on this vessel until it reached Germany where they were interned for the rest of the war.

Colonel Strangman and a small group were placed onboard a captured collier, the *Igotz Mendi* which then proceeded towards Germany via the Baltic.

However the German plans fell away one foggy night when they ran aground near Denmark. Now it was the turn for the Germans to be imprisoned. The Danish authorities marched them away and advised the Australians to make their own way to Britain as quickly as possible. This they eventually succeeded in doing. Colonel Strangman reported that the Germans had treated them well but his health had suffered as the food had been poor. Upon arrival in Britain he put his medical skills to work in England and France. He did not return to his home in Adelaide until December 1918. Those there had assumed he was dead as his obituary notice had appeared a number of times in various newspapers. (4)

Unlike the *AE1* incident this episode had a happy ending. It did however, impact on an already ailing Colonel Pethebridge. He returned to Australia in October, 1917 and died on 25 January, 1918.

An overview of the Royal Australian Naval role; in hindsight

As early as the last month of 1914, criticisms began to emerge over the fact that the RAN had not taken steps to occupy the German islands just north of the equator. These were the Pelew, Marianne, Caroline and Marshall island groups. This task was ultimately carried out by the Japanese Navy.

Even as early as October, 1914 the Australian Naval Board clearly indicated to the British Admiralty "that these islands closely affect the whole question of naval defence of Australia in the future". (5) Such critical opinions were to intensify years later when, in the post-war settlements, Japan was given extensive administrative control over these islands. It reached fever pitch in the lead-up to World War II when the Japanese established a naval base in the area.

The decision not to proceed to the German islands north of the equator was probably the correct one in terms of naval strategy at that time. But it also came as the result of political pressure from the Japanese and British reluctance to offend its naval ally.

Admiral Patey, Commander of the Australian fleet, did not see as his key role proceeding beyond New Guinea once German possessions there had been secured. To him the key objective was to seek out von Spee's German Pacific squadron. If this could be achieved in

Vice Admiral Patey, Commander, RAN 1913–15
AWM: EN0385

conjunction with a sweep of those islands to the north-west, well and good. But in attempting this he would run the risk of failing in his key role and thereby being accused of putting local Australian interests ahead of those of the Empire and its allies.

There were very good reasons why Admiral Patey would see the prime role of the RAN as that of pursuing the German fleet. He was of Royal Navy background and as early as 19th August, 1914 the British Secretary of State for the Colonies had made it clear to the Australian government where they felt the prime Naval role should be focussed. Moreover Admiral Patey had been informed of their views:

"Troops occupying German territory need not anticipate attack by hostile military expeditions carried oversea nor from enemy warships… As His Majesty's ships cannot be continuously employed for protecting coastline of occupied territory it is intended to set warships free for their proper function as soon as military expeditions have been safely conveyed and established at their destination. Admiral is being informed direct by Lords Commissioners of the Admiralty in this sense." (6)

There were also specific factors which endorsed Patey's decision to seek out the German squadron. Both HMAS *Melbourne* and HMAS *Sydney* were due to return to Sydney for a re-fit. There was a shortage of coal at Rabaul. In addition Australian vessels would soon be required to transport troops to Europe.

At the same time the role played by the Japanese Navy had undergone change. The original intention was that its role would not extend beyond the China seas. Just one month later (September, 1914) the British decided to allow them to cruise around the Marianne and Caroline Island groups in order to hunt for Germans ships. In mid-October the Australian government learnt that the Japanese had occupied Yap, in the Caroline Islands. (7) The Naval Board then pointed out to Admiral Patey that the occupation of Yap was one of their own originally-designated tasks. Patey was in agreement with the Australians but could not use the *Berrima* for transport to Yap (as it had reverted to a transport ship), nor the *Encounter* whose draft was too large for the harbour there.

On 23rd October, 1914 a decision was made to arm the *Komet* and the *Fantome*, equip them with RAN personnel and send them as escorts to an expedition "to take possession of Pelew, Marshall, Caroline and Marianne Islands".(8) At this point several factors combined and created an extensive delay, for example, the refitting of the *Komet* and *Fantome.* A month passed.

These delays meant that the achievements of the Japanese Navy filtered back to the Japanese people. They took great pride that their navy had taken various island groups from the powerful Germans. Now they were being asked to hand them over to Australia. Riots broke out in Tokyo. The Japanese brought pressure to bear on the British government. The British hesitated, but ultimately conceded during the last week of November. When Australia asked what was going on they were finally told (on 3rd December) that for "strategic reasons" all four of the northern island groups would be given to Japan to supervise, leaving the "whole question of their future to be settled at the end of the war". The proposed Australian expedition, which even had its stamps over-printed "NW Pacific" was stood down. (9)

None of the problems that arose many years later, would have become an issue, had the Australian expedition proceeded to re-claim these island groups when the decision for them to do so was first made.

The best form of vision is always hindsight...

Chapter 11

MISSION (PARTLY) ACCOMPLISHED

They shall not grow old as we that are left grow old...

(The Ode, Laurence Binyon)

The original task allocated to Australia by the British government was two-fold; to occupy German possessions in New Guinea and the nearby outposts and islands and to hold and administer them for the duration of the war. The Occupation phase of this task had now been achieved (some of the more distant island groups were captured by the Japanese).

The achievement of this military objective had not been a bloodless coup. There had been a total loss of seven lives counting the sole German death. However fighting had not been protracted; aside from the odd angry shot, all of the fighting had been conducted on one day. When this campaign was compared with later World War I battlefields, such as Gallipoli and the Western Front with their vast losses of life, it became easy to see the Australian occupation of New Guinea as nothing more than a skirmish. In fact a certain degree of derision was displayed. In the following article from the *Sydney Morning Herald* the men of the AN&MEF were referred to as “Coconut Lancers”.

"The exploits of the A.E.F. now facetiously referred to as the 'Coconut Lancers', in the light of subsequent events, and later knowledge appear almost Gilbertian, although to the participants it was a matter they regarded as of serious moment, and the fact they were braving dangers which did not actually exist does not in any way detract from their courage or efficiency. Stories are told of how the troops encamped in a coconut plantation imagined themselves surrounded by enemies, who with each succeeding day, were magnified into an army… It was some time before a few long-bearded and venerable missionaries made their way in and explained that there would be no armed resistance." (1)

Aside from the obvious inaccuracies stated in this article it is relevant to note that it was actually an article, not a letter to the Editor written by some disgruntled civilian or former soldier. It was written just as C.E.W. Bean was working with S. S. Mackenzie on the task of finalising the Official War History of the campaign for printing. It drew an immediate and angry response from Bean and when reading his response it is relevant to note that Bean had himself been at Gallipoli and the Western front and so was in a really sound position to comment on the article.

"But anyone who fought in the late war knows, or should know the utter worthlessness of what the AIF called 'furphies'- wild stories and rumours which are believed at the time and, doubtless, if uncontradicted, pass into history. The fact is that the small force which landed at Kabakaul so far from having to face 'dangers which actually did not exist', was plunged into what- whether judged by the standards of Palestine or of the Western Front-was a nasty, sharp, difficult little fight, with several crises which, though fortunately not entailing great loss of life, required to be met with the utmost pluck and determination."

This says it all. The writer of the article should have considered himself told. But Bean did not leave it there:

"It was in this fight that Captain Antill Pockley lost his life, after giving away his Red Cross brassard to protect a stretcher bearer, and founded the magnificent tradition of the medical services of the AIF; and that, at a moment when a small column was facing a deadlock, Commander Elwell led his men in a most gallant charge straight for the German trench, and by his death founded a similar tradition for our navy." (2)

Breaking new ground

At the time that this debate took place (1926) and even today, not many Australians recalled this campaign and among the few who did, details were often only sparsely known. As Charles Bean stated, the men of the AN&MEF were pioneers in Australian military traditions in the sense that they were the first to perform a particular task or take part in a certain event.

In fact the list of achievements and deeds performed by the men of the AN&MEF which were a "first" for the young Australian nation during the Great War is quite extensive, not to mention, impressive. It is not the purpose here to discuss each of them in detail so it will suffice just to point them out. The view that this campaign was Australia's "Real Baptism of Fire" in the sense of its being Australia's first battle in a war which it entered after Federation, will be evaluated later. The "New Ground" achievements were:

1. The first overseas military expedition planned and co-ordinated by the Australian Commonwealth government.
2. The first joint operation by the Australian Army and Navy.
3. When HMAS *Encounter* intercepted and captured the steamer *Zambezi*, (an ex-British vessel under German control), this became the RAN's first wartime prize.
4. The first amphibious landing by Australian wartime forces.
5. The first Australian land operation of World War I.
6. The Australians fighting on the Bitapaka road were the first jungle fighters of World War I.
7. The first shot fired in battle by a member of an Australian military force (when Petty Officer Palmer shot and wounded Sergeant-Major Mauderer).
8. The first recorded act of bravery by an Australian during World War I (when Captain Brian Pockley took off his Red Cross brassard and gave it to Stoker Kember who accompanied the wounded AB Seaman Williams to the rear).
9. The first Australian death during World War I (either Captain Pockley or AB Williams).
10. Lieutenant-Commander Elwell was the first Naval officer, serving with the RAN, to lose his life during World War I (Elwell was actually British but had been serving with the RAN).

11. Lieutenant-Commander Elwell had died with his sword in hand leading a bayonet charge. This was the first bayonet charge by Australians against Germany in their own territory.
12. Lieutenant Bowen was the first Australian officer to lead his troops in to action in enemy territory and the first Australian officer to be wounded.
13. HMAS *Encounter* fired the first offensive shots by the RAN during World War I when it shelled the ridges near Toma.
14. The loss of the first RAN vessel during a period of hostilities although, according to the opinion of most, not due to those hostilities; the *AE1*.

What an impressive list of achievements! Website research has shown that the Royal Australian Navy lays particular claim to those achievements listed under Point numbers 3 and 13, both of which involve HMAS *Encounter*. The Naval Historical Society, based at Garden Island Sydney, also lays claim to these two points and, in addition, Points 1 and 2, 4 through to 6, 8, 10 as well as 11 and 12. (3)

Charles Bean was meticulous in pursuing even the smallest of details concerning the events which unfolded in New Guinea in 1914. In 1934 (twenty years after the landing at Kabakaul) he wrote to RAAF Wing Commander Harrison:

"In looking through some of the early war records of the Defence Department, I see that a flight of the Australian Flying Corps, comprising yourself and Lieutenant Mars, with two machines (a B.2a and a Farman waterplane) left Australia for service with the expedition to New Guinea on November, 1914... I would be grateful if you could let me know whether these machines reached New Guinea and, if so, whether they ever flew there." (4)

Apparently at various times Government ministers had claimed that this was the first time that a Flying unit had gone abroad for service against the enemy. Bean was trying to verify the truth of this claim. Some three months later he was informed that two planes, one a land biplane and the other a sea plane, both with 70 HP Renault engines, had in fact, been shipped to New Guinea on 30 November, 1914. However:

"The planes were not assembled as, the purpose for which they had been sent did not exist at the time of their arrival, i.e. spotting some enemy vessel that had been in the vicinity at the time and the cost of fitting them up would have been about 700 pounds." (5)

As a result the planes were simply shipped back to Australia. Had that not been the outcome then perhaps yet another first may well have been notched up.

Counting the cost… further evaluation

Casualties among the Australians were two officers and four men killed with one officer and three men wounded. On the German side the casualties were officially reported as one white non-commissioned officer (Sergeant Ritter) and 30 native officers killed with one white non-commissioned officer (Sergeant-Major Mauderer) and 10 native soldiers wounded. The numbers given by the Germans were stated as "approximate", presumably referring to losses among the native soldiers.

Taken as prisoners were three officers, 16 white non-commissioned officers and 56 native troops. Many native soldiers fled into the bush and some of these later made their way back to Toma. (6)

The campaign must be seen as a military victory as it did achieve the original aim; to take from Germany its colonial possessions in New Guinea. This fact remains despite the fact that the fatalities among the Australians were greater than those of their adversaries.

Opinions differ as to whether the campaign could have been managed better. S.S. Mackenzie, who wrote about this campaign as part of C.E.W. Bean's Official History of World War I, gave a brief and quite balanced summary. He pointed out that whilst the native troops had the advantage of cover and prepared defence positions, they were not up to the task of dealing with disciplined and determined troops. There is also the inescapable fact that the Australian forces far outnumbered the German defensive forces. Admittedly only a fraction of the invading force was actually deployed to the battle area, but the fact remains that reserves were there had they been needed. They weren't.

Mackenzie also points out that the Germans, in their official report, admitted that they had underestimated the ability of the Australians to fight in thick bush. Nor had they expected them to enter the bush to outflank them; they had expected them to simply move up the road. (7)

Some claims were made that the Germans had placed native soldiers up trees from where they could snipe at the advancing Australians. Charles Bean spent some time investigating these claims and decided that there was no basis to them. One native was placed up a tree as a lookout; his task was to signal for the landmines to be detonated. Bean also investigated the claim by some that the Germans were firing dum dum bullets. He found this to be false. (8)

However there were also those who critical of the battle tactics. It is valid to ask why a lightly-armed naval party was the first to be deployed when there also existed the decisive firepower of a machine gun unit. Most likely Admiral Patey was able to persuade Colonel Holmes to let the Navy have the first crack. In hindsight it is somewhat easy to see this as a poor tactical decision. On the other hand it may have been better for the machine gunners to have been brought forward earlier, once it was realised just how well entrenched and hidden were the German defenders.

One member of the machine section that had been put ashore with Lieutenant-Commander Elwell was particularly critical of the way in which the naval men had earlier advanced up the Bitapaka road. In his view no scouts were sent in advance and given that the road had in fact been mined, any advance up the road itself was tantamount to suicide. AB Seaman Billy Williams was shot whilst advancing in this manner. It is possible that this criticism, coming from a member of the militia, may simply have been motivated by rivalry between the two branches of the Australian defence forces involved in New Guinea. Apparently the military members of the expeditionary force were somewhat disappointed when the decision was made to give the senior service the chance to make the opening advance.

This viewpoint itself raises the question... Why was so much of the activity which took place on that day (11th September, 1914) left to members of the Naval reserves whilst the militia were considerably less involved? No clear-cut answer seems to have emerged but there have been suggestions made as to why this happened. Some border on innuendo; few seem to be grounded in fact. They do help explain why this campaign was, at times, later described in a derisive manner. It may also help explain why it is less well-known.

Brave deeds

Mention has been made of Captain Pockley's action of giving his Red Cross arm-band to Kember when he escorted the wounded Williams to the rear. Some have felt that in doing so he contributed to his own death by removing his identification as a medical officer. It is also true to say that the native officers, often in a state of near panic, were firing so frequently that Captain Pockley would still have become a victim. Captain Pockley's action was an unselfish one; he was doing his best to ensure the survival of Williams and Kember. After all that was his appointed task. He was there as a doctor; not a combatant.

There is no definitive answer as to which of the two men initially wounded, AB Seaman Williams or Captain Pockley, was the first to succumb to their wounds.

"It is commonly believed that, because Williams was shot first, he was the first to die. However, one report from the "Berrima" puts Williams' death at 2:50pm and Captain Pockley's at 2pm." (9)

In the final analysis this is not a major issue. What is more important is the fact that two families, (and many more to come over the remaining years of the war), were left devastated by the loss of a loved one. From a discussion with Simon Pockley, a descendant of Captain Brian Pockley's Father, this writer learnt that members of the Pockley family and descendants of Billy Williams, gather on 11th September each year at the Shrine of Remembrance in Melbourne to commemorate their deaths. The Northcote RSL Club also acknowledges this occasion.

Captain Elwell's charge towards the enemy trench was a brave but also a somewhat foolhardy deed. An act of bravado which was to

AB Seaman Billy Williams
AWM: P04124.001

be repeated endlessly in the remaining years of World War I. It took far too long for those in charge to realise that the tactics which were successful in by-gone wars were less likely to succeed against men well concealed and with fast-firing machine guns or even, for that matter, men armed with rifles.

There is no doubt that Lieutenant Bowen showed great initiative and good leadership. His use of a captured German officer as a shield/ message bearer was perhaps, technically, an infringement of the rules of war but a minor one; it paled into insignificance in terms of what was to come later in the war. The use of gas, by both sides on the Western Front, comes to mind. As he himself said and as discussed earlier, his actions achieved their objective and in doing so actually saved lives rather than adding to the cost. At any rate no charges were ever made against Lieutenant Bowen and nor should they have been.

It is also perhaps the case that the Australians were at times favoured by good fortune. One such case was the manner in which they discovered the planted dynamite mines. Had the native delegated as a lookout not lost his cool they may never have learnt of the existence of the mines. The consequences would have been disastrous.

Earlier they had walked right through some Germans waiting in ambush. Fortunately they were spotted by Petty Officer Palmer who shot Mauderer in the hand thereby foiling a potential and deadly ambush.

There is no escaping the fact that sheer bravery and determination played a major role in the ultimate success of this, Australia's first military foray into enemy territory. Whilst Lieutenant Bond was the only man to receive a military decoration (Distinguished Service Order) for bravery performed on the Bitapaka road, there were several of those involved who were mentioned in despatches.

The citation for Bond's DSO reads as follows:

"On 11th September 1914, during the attack upon the Wireless station, Bita Paka, German New Guinea, Lieutenant Bond displayed conspicuous ability and coolness under fire in leading his men through most difficult country and enforcing the terms of surrender whilst drawing off an attack by another body of the enemy. He showed great daring, when accompanied by only one officer and one man, in suddenly disarming 8 Germans in the presence of 20 German native troops drawn up under arms, all of whom were then marched off and held prisoners. Later he personally captured 5 armed natives." (10)

Those mentioned in despatches for their contribution during this battle were:

- Captain Reginald John Albert Travers, A.M.F.
- Captain Brian Colden Antill Pockley, A.A.M.C. (killed in action).
- Commander, later Captain, Claude Lionel Cumberlege, R.N.
- Commander Joseph Arthur Hamilton Beresford, R.A.N.
- Lieutenant-Commander Charles Bingham Elwell, R.N. (killed in action).
- Lieutenant Rowland Griffith Bowen, R.A.N.
- Lieutenant Gerald Ashby Hill, R.A.N.
- Midshipman Reginald Langdon Buller, R.A.N.R.
- Gunner George Alfred Stevens, R.N.
- Gunner (later Acting Mate) Samuel Thomas Percy Yeo, R.N.
- Gunner Charles Frederick Bacon, R.N.
- Petty Officer Frederick Robert Sandys, R.N., ON 192834.
- Petty Officer G.R. Palmer, R.A.N.R.
- Petty Officer Archibald Edward Bones, R.N. ON 199133 (R.F.R. Chatham B8212). (11)

The Fallen

The complete list of those members of the AN&MEF who died during the attack and key background details, where known and not previously stated, is as follows:

Officers:

- **Captain Brian Colden Antill Pockley. A.A.M.C.**
  Born St. Leonards, Sydney, 4 June 1890.
- **Lieutenant-Commander Charles Bingham Elwell.**
  R.N. Born Albrighton, Shropshire, England, 13 September, 1882.

Other Ranks:

Able Seaman William G.V. Williams,

No. 4 Company Naval Reserves. His date of birth unknown but Billy Williams was aged 28 at the time of his death. Billy had lived with his mother and sister at 36 Beavers Road, Northcote, Victoria. He had served five years in the Naval Reserve and had previously worked as an engine room attendant at the Melbourne Electricity Supply Company. (12).

Able Seaman Harry W. Street. R.A.N.R.

Very few details are known apart from the fact that he was a labourer, 32 years old in August, 1914 and five foot four inches tall. Harry Street did have a poem dedicated to his memory. Here is an extract from the poem *The Soldier's Sleep*, written by "Target".

"Street has gone to sleep,
He will not wake again:
He will not laugh, nor weep,
Nor pleasure know, nor pain." (13)

Signalman R.D. Moffatt. Engineer of Kensington, Sydney, NSW.

Born Lostwithiel, Cornwall, England, December,1894. (14)

Able Seaman John Courtney. R.A.N.R.

Real name John Edward Walker. Born Ross Island, Townsville, Queensland, 1885. He had once used his godmother's surname of Courtney to get a job on a ship. As his discharge papers were made out in the name of Courtney he continued to use this name when applying for work. He joined the Navy in 1905, serving as a fulltime sailor for five years before joining the Naval Reserve. He lived at Bank Street, North Sydney with his parents and his wife and had worked on a station at Walgett, NSW. (15).

Rabaul Military Cemetery at Rabaul
AWM: H15076

The burials

Most, but not all, of those killed at Kabakaul were interred at two different locations. Lieutenant-Commander Elwell, AB Seaman Courtney and AB Seaman Street were hit during the heat of battle, died almost instantly and were buried near to where they were hit.

Captain Pockley and AB Seaman Williams were both badly wounded and later carried aboard HMAS *Berrima* where they later died. Late in the afternoon of the day of the assault their bodies were carried ashore, wrapped in the Union Jack. Members of the Army Medical Corps and Naval reservists then carried them to the cemetery at Herbertshohe. Here the pall bearers and about twelve officers took part in a service conducted by Chaplain Little.

The bodies of all five of these men were later exhumed. On 11 July, 1919 they made their last journey aboard HMAS *Una* from Kabakaul to the Rabaul cemetery where they were re-interred with "full Naval and Military honours." (16).

Captain Pockley's father, Dr. Francis Pockley, did not learn about the re-interment until sometime after it occurred. In a letter of 25th September, 1919 he stated that had he known that his son's body was to be exhumed he would have asked for him to be returned home for burial in the family burial ground. There was also a problem, created by a bureaucratic bungle, with the way in which they had spelt Captain Pockley's name on the headstone. Several letters passed between Dr. Francis Pockley senior and Army records before the spelling was amended from "Brien" to the correct spelling of "Brian". (17). Remembrance with respect does indeed involve getting the spelling correct.

Able Seaman Robert Moffatt was also carried aboard HMAS *Berrima* after he was wounded. He died the next day, after the burial of Captain Pockley and AB Seaman Williams. He was buried at sea.

It is somewhat of a sad postscript that the man about whom the least is known does not have a land-based burial site.

AB Seaman Robert Moffatt
AWM: J00510

The wounded

Officer: Lieutenant Rowland Griffiths Bowen.

Born 14 January, 1879 at Tagerty, Victoria.

Grew up in Petrie, Queensland. Married to Agnes Grace Mary Bell 14 August, 1914. Worked as a clerk on the railways in Brisbane before joining the Queensland Naval Brigade. Joined the R.A.N. as a Lieutenant. Served as District Naval Officer on Thursday Island until February 1914 and then in the same role in Melbourne until the outbreak of war.

Details on his post-New Guinea career will be given in a later chapter, along with others from the AN&MEF who went on to long and distinguished careers. (18)

Other Ranks:

AB Seaman Daniel Sillars Skillen.
Born Ardrossan, Scotland. R.A.N.R.

Worked as a labourer and lived in at 64 Gipps Street, Balmain at the time when he successfully applied for a War Gratuity. He was discharged as unfit for further service. He married on 28th February, 1919. (19)

AB Seaman Timothy Sullivan.
Born London 5th February, 1877.

Labourer of Upper Mitcham, South Australia. AB Sullivan suffered multiple wounds and played no further part in the war effort apart from speaking at a number of recruitment rallies. Upon receiving sustained applause at a rally in Victor Harbour (19 August 1915) he modestly proclaimed that "my pals at the Dardanelles deserve that sort of thing better than I do." (20)

AB Seaman James Henry Tonks.
Born Port Adelaide, 14th September, 1880.

Labourer. 6th September, 1915 he joined the AIF and served on the Western Front as a Gunner. In the second half of 1917 he received a gunshot wound in the right leg. He was declared permanently unfit for war service and returned to Australia in September, 1918. He was awarded an Invalid pension but continued to suffer hardship. He walked with a permanent limp and he and his wife struggled to raise their five children. For a while he was involved with his brothers in his father's carrying business. (21)

There can be no doubt that for AB Seaman Tonks and many others similarly mistreated by the "Fortunes of War", Life had not turned out for them as they had envisaged when they enlisted.

This raises the question… do we really do enough to remember them?

Chapter 12

GERMAN DEFIANCE... A ONE-MAN WAR?

I think a hero is an ordinary individual
who finds strength to
persevere and endure in spite of
overwhelming obstacles.

(Christopher Reeve)

Following World War II, after the Allies had swept the Japanese forces back across the south-west Pacific region, stories began to emerge of defiant Japanese soldiers hiding themselves in the jungle, determined to fight on and never surrender. Not many people realise that a generation earlier, a German soldier, in the jungles of the New Guinea mainland, was similarly defiant in the face of defeat. Similar, but not identical.

Captain Hermann Detzner was more of an explorer and a scientist than a fanatical soldier bent on "death before dishonour". He acted more from Prussian stubbornness and patriotism than from fervent loyalty to a revered, god-like Emperor. Other key differences existed but there was one significant similarity between Detzner and the Japanese; a refusal to surrender.

When war broke out Detzner was on mainland New Guinea conducting a survey of the border between the German territory and British New Guinea. He was accompanied by Sergeant Konradt and a large party of New Guinean soldiers and carriers. Concerns had arisen over the fact that gold prospectors had been crossing the border and so his task was to clearly define where it lay.

The Australians became aware of the presence of Detzner and his party in October, 1914. George Chisholm, officer-in-charge of the Lakekamu goldfield set out to track him down. Coming upon a small group of Germans led by Sergeant Konradt, Chisholm decided to follow them. One of the New Guineans fell ill and was left behind with a stretcher party. Chisholm caught up with this group, imprisoned the fit men and left the sick man with a note to give to his superiors. The note advised the Germans to go to the Nepa camp at the Lakekamu goldfield to surrender.

Surrender there with all your men. You will be treated as an officer and a gentleman.
Chisholm,
Officer in charge of The British Force. (1)

The note was retrieved by Konradt when he returned to the area. Unfortunately the New Guinea native had died. Konradt was not able to read English so he took Chisholm's note to Captain Detzner. Always the defiant patriot, Detzner set off in pursuit of the Australians with the intention of attacking them. After failing to locate them he headed for the coast.

Travel for Detzner and his party now became quite a daring adventure. He travelled by raft down the Watut to its junction with the Markham River and on to the Lutheran mission station near to where the

Nadzab International Airport is today. Here he was told that the Morobe Station was still in German hands. Detzner decided to head for Morobe via the Lutheran mission at Burgberg (Lae today). Here he was given the use of the mission schooner Bavaria for the trip to Morobe. Unfortunately for Detzner, the schooner foundered but a friendly chief came to his aid by lending his party a big sea-going canoe. By the time he reached the Lutheran station at Malalo most of the native police had deserted. It was at Malalo that Konradt and another German, Banik, fell ill with malaria. These two remained behind. On 26th February, 1915 they were captured by an Australian patrol and subsequently sent to Australia for internment.

By this time, any ideas Detzner may have had of attacking the Australians would have disappeared. So he decided to disappear himself by making for the neutral Netherlands New Guinea. He also knew that the Australians were now actively looking for him. Detzner and his companion Klink, made for Singaua Plantation, east of Burgberg and set up camp. Once again the Australians arrived in the area. During the first weeks of March, 1915, Klink decided "enough was enough" and so he surrendered leaving Detzner to strive alone to maintain his freedom. Detzner continued his "boys own" adventures and headed for Finschhafen.

Still stubborn and defiant Detzner had no plans to surrender. His only support was a few loyal native police and carriers. Most men would have given up. But Detzner once again received assistance. He had climbed to Sattelberg, the Lutheran mission station overlooking Finschhafen. Here the veteran missionary and explorer, Christian Keyyser felt that, as a Christian, it was his duty to come to Detzner's aid. This was a difficult situation for Keyyser as it would mean not only defying the Australians and their insistence on neutrality but also disobeying his superior. The problem was resolved when the local natives provided food and shelter for Detzner who, in return, agreed not to make any attack upon the Australians. Keyyser, in turn, promised to keep Detzner's location a secret. (1)

Detzner remained at this location for the remainder of the war. From time to time he moved about to nearby places, singing patriotic songs and raising the German flag before returning to Sattelberg. Episodes such as these would have provided a break in Detzner's routine which must have become tedious at times.

There does not appear to have been any occasion when Detzner and his group actually engaged or attacked the Australians. However he did retain a loyal following. The Australians knew broadly of his whereabouts and claimed to have even spotted him from afar. They threatened to burn the villages of those who harboured him and his men. Occasionally the Germans would glean snippets of information of the progress of the war. There were a number of occasions when his New Guinean companions would endeavour to persuade him to surrender. For Detzner surrender was not an option.

Detzner was to make a lot of claims about his exploits in a book he wrote after the war. He stated that he had made three attempts to reach Netherlands New Guinea. The main attempt was made in 1916 along the southern slopes of the Bismarck range. Before turning back (many of his carriers were nearing exhaustion or suffering from ulcers or rheumatism) he recorded that he had reached a point west of the 145th meridian which, if true, meant he was the first white man to view the valleys of the Highlands. (2)

So the war passed by Hermann Detzner. He kept his word not to attack the Australians. His battles were with the diseases and environment of the New Guinea mainland. In many ways, given his scientific background, his exploits were of greater benefit to all nations, not just the greater glory of his homeland.

Word of the signing of the Armistice reached Finschhafen on a New Guinea Company vessel on the day we now know as Remembrance Day. Christian Keyyser sent a mission worker to Detzner with a letter confirming the news. Ten days later, (21st November, 1918) Detzner wrote to District Officer Nelson offering to surrender. The Deputy District Officer, Captain M.J. Millane was dispatched from Morobe with a detachment of native police.

Attired in full-dress but tattered military uniform, complete with sun helmet and sword, Hermann Detzner met them at Finschhafen and formally surrendered. The Australians treated him with complete respect, initially allowing him to continue to wear his uniform. He was held in Morobe until 22nd December before embarking on the Sumatra bound for Rabaul, arriving on 5 January, 1919. He was not allowed to wear his uniform there because of concern over the possibility of a negative reaction from angry Australians.

Those who made that decision need not have worried. In fact the Australians were somewhat in awe of Detzner and his exploits. On the voyage to Rabaul he was invited to have drinks and also dined with the Australian officers. Finally he was put onboard *SS Melissa*, bound for Australia on the 31st January, 1919. After a period of internment at Liverpool he was repatriated to Germany. Here he was greeted warmly. He wrote a book about his exploits and discoveries and upon its publication in 1921 he became a celebrity.

It is possible that during his years of voluntary "internment", isolation… call it what you will… Hermann Detzner contributed more to science and exploration than he did to the German war effort. But even here Detzner became a controversial figure. When his book was first published his claims about geographical discoveries were taken at face value. He was later awarded the prestigious Nachtigal Medal by the German Geographical Society. As time went by it appeared that many of his claims were fictitious. They were subjected to much scrutiny and criticism. Foremost among those critics was Christain Keyyser, the Lutheran missionary, who had "turned a blind eye" to Detzner's presence. He was also a genuine explorer and many claims made by Detzner actually related to achievements by Keyyser. (3)

But can Detzner's refusal to surrender be compared to the defiance and fervor of the Japanese soldiers isolated at the end of World War II? Not really!

Detzner made no attack upon Australian occupying forces. It was claimed by some that he tied up large numbers of enemy soldiers who were sent in search of him. Whether or not this is true is really a moot point. These soldiers were based in New Guinea anyway and had not been diverted from theatres of war.

Nor did the Japanese soldiers have the assistance afforded to Hermann Detzner. Initially the party travelling with Detzner was quite substantial. Disease and illness, exhaustion and lack of commitment, slowly whittled away the numbers of his group until such time as he alone remained. But he always had the covert assistance of loyal natives, patriotic fellow Germans or compassionate missionaries.

He even had access to medical supplies with which to combat illness or disease should the need arise. Unlike the Japanese, Detzner could stop and rest. He could put his feet up, secure in the knowledge that no one would accidentally stumble upon his hideaway. In fact Detzner was warned, at various times, that his enemy was nearby. The Japanese soldiers hidden away at war's end acted alone, unassisted and were obliged to be ever-vigilant. As an officer who had served in New Guinea for some time prior to the war, Detzner had a greater knowledge of the local landscape than did the Japanese. He was, after all, a surveyor as well as a soldier.

Whilst Detzner was not endowed with the same fanaticism of the Japanese soldier-recluses he did share their determination. He remained defiant to the last...and beyond the war. In November 1919 whilst lecturing to the Berlin Geographical Society he put forward arguments as to why he believed Australia should not be allowed control over New Guinea affairs. He argued that military levies there had developed into slave hunts and claimed that even English plantation owners had written letters to him advocating that the country should not be handed over to Australia. (4)

This came at a time when the whole issue of establishing protectorates over the former German colonial possessions in New Guinea was under discussion both within Australia and at the League of Nations. When the *Argus* (Melbourne) reported Detzner's views the response was immediate. A letter, signed *Rabaul and France 1914-19*, denied that Australian plantation owners had been cruel. (5)

Exception was also taken to Detzner's opinion that he had outsmarted all efforts to capture him. It was stated that his movements were always well known by the District Officers at Morobe and that Detzner had survived on rations supplied by the South Australian Lutheran Mission despite the fact that each and every one had signed an oath of neutrality. (6)

It is debatable as to whether or not Detzner and his band of men were really that serious a thorn in the side of the Australian forces. There is, however, little doubt that his exploits were considerably daring in their nature. He showed an enormous amount of determination in sticking to his initial resolution… even if it was assisted by sympathetic supporters.

Chapter 13

GERMAN RESENTMENT... ROUGH JUSTICE

"Vengeance is mine; I will repay, saith the Lord."

(Romans 12:19)

A matter of weeks after the Terms of Surrender had been signed an incident occurred which was to test Holmes' abilities yet again. It arose as the result of a mix of alcohol and the surly and resentful demeanour of those drinking it. Significantly, the incident occurred just as the Australians were trying to assert their control but actually happened well away from where that control was strongest.

The drinking session took place on 26th October, 1914 at the isolated outpost of Namatanai in New Ireland. At that point in time Namatanai had not been occupied by Australian troops. Those involved were German civilians and a Belgian planter. As was the case with many among the German community there was a certain degree of paranoia as to how they would be treated by the victors. There was also considerable resentment that Germany was the vanquished.

As the drinking progressed, conversation began to focus on the activities of one Reverend William Henry Cox, a British Methodist missionary, and the German schooner *Samoa* which had gone into hiding when the AN&MEF had arrived. The drinking group became aware that Cox had received a letter from a fellow British citizen onboard the *Samoa*, urging Cox to alert the British authorities as to where the vessel lay hiding. Without evidence of any kind the Germans "tried" Cox (in his absence) and found him to be guilty of being a spy.

The gathered group had detected a growing restlessness among the native population since the arrival of the Australians and so they were keen to stop that restlessness from spreading. Having adopted this viewpoint it was an easy step from there to identify Cox and his fellow missionaries as scapegoats. They were accused of fomenting rebellion amongst the natives. As some German planters lived some distance from the white community they dreaded the possibility of a native insurrection.

Two unfortunate circumstances arose, basically by chance, to further inflame the already potentially volatile situation. An envelope bearing a letter for Cox fell into the hands of the incensed drinkers. They wrongly interpreted the stamped seal on it to be that of the British Navy. At the same time, Dr. Braunert, the German medical Officer, heard that Cox was in the area. Dr. Braunert returned to Namatanai from the mission station he had been visiting and went to District Officer Bruckner's house. Bruckner was preparing to leave the area so as to avoid having to surrender to the Australians. Resentful, Braunert then joined the group of drinkers.

So here was Braunert, drinking with a group of equally resentful Germans just at the time that the one person who should have and maybe would have restrained them, had left the district. In fact, as he left, Bruckner did try to warn Cox that trouble was brewing. But this was to prove to be of no avail. Dr. Braunert had already suggested to the group that Cox deserved a good thrashing. Three of the group, Hornung, Koster and Phillips declined to get involved. They pointed out that Cox could claim he was beaten simply because he was British. Braunert was insistent and was able to persuade them to attend as witnesses.

By this time all members of the group were quite drunk but that didn't stop them from setting off in search of Cox. One of the group, Hoepfel, was left behind as he had fallen into a drunken sleep. However their numbers were bolstered as they travelled because they met up with Dr. Braunert's young assistant, Otto Paul, who Braunert was able to co-opt into joining them even though he was barely aware of what was going on. Paul later tried to justify his decision by saying that he did not want to be seen as a coward by the group and that he thought the target of their anger was some disobedient natives.

Upon arrival at the mission station three of the group burst into the mission house where Cox sat talking to the missionary's wife. Dr Braunert, brandishing a pistol, exclaimed, "You are a prisoner".

Cox was dragged outside onto the verandah and down the steps. Once there, Cox was firmly held over a washtub and given between 30 and 40 strokes with a cane. The missionary returned just in time to see the attackers running away.

Badly bruised and in considerable pain, Cox, with the help of a native guide made his way across the island to Labor where he boarded the mission schooner, *Litia*, for the journey to Rabaul, via Ulu. Upon arrival he reported the thrashing to Colonel Holmes and subjected himself to an examination of the bruises by Colonel Maguire[1], the Principal Medical Officer.

1 Colonel FA Maguire, CMG, DSO, V.D., A.DMS, 3rd Aust. Div. 1918/20, Medical Practitioner of Sydney, b. Cobar, NSW, 28 March, 1888.

Holmes immediately set in motion a set of responses, not all of which were the result of a correct and proper decision. He dispatched Major Ralston and a force of 25 men to arrest the perpetrators. He also directed his chief judicial officer, Captain Charles Manning, to conduct an inquiry. Captain Manning visited Namatanai, interviewed the missionary and his wife and obtained admissions of guilt from those attackers whom he was able to apprehend there.

Manning's investigations were thorough and carried out efficiently and quickly. This was facilitated by the frank admissions of those accused. But they were not conducted in the manner of a courtroom trial. This situation was to later have significant consequences.

He handed in his report on 28th November, just over a month after the thrashing had occurred. It clearly indicated that Dr. Braunert was the ringleader; Hornung, Koster and Phillips, although not actively involved were deemed to be accomplices. Conversely the young assistant, Paul, was seen as an active participant but one who took part because of his subservience to Braunert. Another German, Wienard, was also seen as guilty but as yet had not been apprehended.

Holmes wasted no time in deciding the fate of the offenders. That same day he issued a proclamation, part of which states:

"In view of the indignity and humiliation inflicted upon the Reverend Mr Cox, a British subject, whose calling as a minister of religion alone should have protected him from such an attack, I consider it necessary that a short, sharp, and exemplary punishment should be meted out to those concerned. The case is a unique one, and must, therefore, be dealt with in a special manner, and I can see no better means of doing this than by awarding the guilty persons a taste of the same medicine they administered to the Reverend Mr Cox."

"I therefore direct that a parade of all available troops of the Rabaul and Herbertshohe garrison be held on Monday next 30th November, in Proclamation square, at 10am, and that the following punishments be publicly inflicted upon the prisoners..."(1)

The proclamation then went on to prescribe 30 strokes of the cane for Dr. Braunert, 25 each for Hornung, Koster and Phillips whilst Otto Paul was to receive 10 strokes of the cane. Wienard's punishment was deferred until such time as he was apprehended. All prisoners were to be deported to Australia on the steamship *Marinda* once the punishment was completed.

Holmes' organisation for this public caning was meticulous and pointed. All local Catholic and Methodist missionaries were invited to attend. The troops were to be formed up around Proclamation square. All German residents were ordered to attend but they were under no actual obligation to stay and watch the caning itself. As a result all but two left when the caning began. The Germans protested against the proceedings by resigning from their official posts.

Holmes also proclaimed that:

"...all natives, including the Police, are to be confined to their quarters between the hours of 9:45am and 10:45am on the 30th instant." (2)

Nor were the members of the Asian community obliged to attend. Apparently the prevailing attitude of the day was that it was not conducive to good government control for subject peoples to be able to witness the flogging of a white man by another white man.

Few would have seen this announcement as racist. Some saw the punishment as unnecessarily harsh. More importantly... there were those who saw the whole response by the Australian authorities as lacking in justice.

Flogging a German offender.
AWM: A026308

Holmes felt that the punishment should fit the crime. The Germans saw it differently. Two Germans spoke to Holmes just before the punishments were inflicted. It is believed that they were pleading with him to imprison the offenders rather than flog them. Holmes refused; he stood firm.

Dr. Maguire, the Australian Principal Medical Officer, examined all of the offenders before the floggings were administered and concluded that all were fit and able to withstand the punishment. Yet when Dr. Braunert was brought forward for punishment he noticed a "small cut about one inch long on the wrist above the radial artery. It did not penetrate the skin." Was this an accident or an attempt to avoid the punishment? (3)

Other preparations were made. The instrument of punishment was a cane, about as thick as one's thumb and four feet long which had previously been used by a German plantation owner to flog disobedient natives. (4)

Colonel Holmes also decided that cameras were not to be taken to the square; Dr. Maguire was not sure whether this direction was given in writing or just verbally. Either way he was not successful as quite a few photographs were taken. Some of these were even taken by the men of the AN&MEF as they stood on the parade ground. Apparently some men had cameras slung around their necks and partly concealed by their shirts; their fellow soldiers helped them conceal their secretive photographic efforts.

It wasn't long before the photographs were turned into postcards and sold around the islands for threepence. Photographs also appeared from other sources. A German civilian had taken some; others ended up in a Brisbane newspaper office. An American fireman from a steamer which happened to be in Rabaul that day took some pictures. He later sold the negatives to the German Consul at Sourabaya for a considerable price. (5)

Within a short time Wienand was apprehended. He, too, received 25 strokes. Holmes may well have considered the matter closed. It wasn't.

On 25th December, 1914, the matter was raised in the Australian Federal Parliament by Senator Millen, the former Defence Minister. The next day the Defence Minister, Senator Pearce, investigated the matter. He found that the inquiry had not been conducted in a courtroom.

In reality the Australian government was probably more concerned about the fact that the incident had gained widespread international attention than they were about the legalities of the matter. The German government saw the propaganda value in using the floggings as a means of gaining sympathy. They told the American ambassador that although they "disapproved most strongly" of the thrashing of Reverend Cox, the offenders deserved "milder judgement". (6) The floggings had occurred at a time when the Allied governments were using propaganda as a means of stimulating recruitment. They had been presenting the Germans as essentially evil. And here were the Australians by-passing proper legal procedures.

The Australian government's inquiry concluded that the floggings were justified because the attack on the Reverend Cox had been a breach of martial law. In addition, Colonel Holmes had been dealing with a dangerous situation as evidenced by the use of weapons and the part played by excessive consumption of alcohol. Furthermore, the German District Officer, Bruckner, although found not guilty of any offence, had known what was about to happen as he had tried to get a warning to the Reverend Cox.

Therefore, the government took no action against Colonel Holmes. They felt that he had been trying to deter others from taking such actions. However, the government did clearly direct that corporal punishment was not to be used again.

In the same month that the Germans had thrashed the Reverend Cox, other floggings had been carried out by the Australians. On a number of occasions, Holmes' son, Basil, had ordered floggings of offending native boys. There had been little disapproval from any in the white community, either German or otherwise.

Such were the attitudes of that time. But it is also a reflection of the fact that this form of punishment on natives had a legal basis under existing (German) territorial law. These laws were still in place in New Guinea as the Australians were occupying the area; they had not annexed it. (7)

Chapter 14

AUSTRALIANS AS ADMINISTRATORS: DIFFICULT ISSUES

"A nation's greatness is measured by how it treats its weakest members."

(Mahatma Gandhi)

Colonel Holmes had originally been charged with the tasks of taking control of German New Guinea and its outposts from the Germans AND administering the former German Protectorate for the duration of the war. The first part of that task, the overthrow of German control, was essentially achieved in mid-September 1914 and fully completed during the remainder of that same year.

Holmes now had to focus on the task of administering the former German possessions, knowing that this duty in no way meant Australia was assured of gaining permanent control over the area at the end of the war. His administration was to take the form of a military administration. This system was to allow control to be in the hands of one man, subject to the supervision of the Australian, and, ultimately, the British governments. As was the case under Germany, there was to be no structure formally representing the views of those being governed.

If the hostilities in and around Rabaul had been Australia's "Baptism of Fire", then the Australian administration of New Guinea during World War I could (in very broad terms and with some poetic licence) be seen as its initiation into the world of colonial control. A "Clayton's" (pseudo) form of colonial control. If you like, a "baptism of administration" of the affairs of another region.

Such a comparison may be going too far but it is true to say that the next four to five years were a totally new experience, in terms of external affairs, for the fledgling nation. It is also true to say that the consequences of these experiences were more long-term for Australia than was the impact of the actual fighting which had already taken place. Australia was to gain control over the New Guinea area after the war under a Protectorate set up and supervised by the League of Nations. Australia remained closely involved with New Guinean affairs right through to the 1970s, when New Guinea gained its independence, and even beyond then because of its geographical proximity to Australia.

Changing of the guard

The men of the AN&MEF had signed up for a six month period. They had successfully completed their appointed task; New Guinea was no longer under German control. It was time for them to be relieved and head home. They were to be replaced with others whose role it was to assist with the administration and security of the former German possessions for the duration of the war.

Colonel Holmes departed New Guinea on 9th January, 1915. A day earlier Colonel Pethebridge formally took over control from

Colonel Holmes. Pethebridge was to continue as Administrator until his death on 25th January, 1918. His position was subsequently filled by Brigadier- General G.J. Johnston on 21st April, 1918. Brigadier-General Johnston was in turn replaced by Brigadier-General T. Griffiths on 1st May, 1920 and the last Administrator under a military occupation, Brigadier-General E.A.Wisdom, was appointed on 6th April, 1921.

The next day the Commonwealth of Australia received a League of Nations Mandate for the government of New Guinea and one month later the military occupation of New Guinea came to an end.

The initial changeover did not go as smoothly as expected partly due to transportation problems associated with getting the men back to Australia. There also existed an underlying tension between the higher ranking members of the departing AN&MEF and that of the incoming group, which was to be known as *Tropical Force.*

Some 34 men of the AN&MEF left for home on 5th January, 1915. A further 260 returned with Holmes when he left on 9th January; 53 departed on 14 January and the largest group (726) were repatriated on 10th February, 1915. 727 men out of this total of 1073 (71%) subsequently re-enlisted in the AIF Finally, 313 men of the naval forces returned home on the *Navua*. Many of those men who joined the AIF later went on to serve at Gallipoli. (1)

The other ranks were generally quite keen to return home but for some of their officers there was a certain degree of anxiety and tension. Some of Holmes' men felt that, as they had captured the former German territory, it was their prerogative to continue and to carry out whatever tasks remained to be done. Those who did remain in office were somewhat apprehensive that the new Administrator would give preferential treatment to his own men. On the other hand, the men of

Colonel Pethebridge
AWM: A02667

the Tropical Force often held the view it was now their turn to lead.

Amongst Holmes' men there was no protracted ill-feeling towards the new administrator, nor was there any overt lack of discipline or disloyalty. It was more a case of "attitude" rather than "action" and it was never prolonged. There was some unpleasantness on the occasion of the departure of some of the occupying troops when, in an effort to curtail looting, the decision was made to search their baggage. The tensions soon passed.

From Holmes' force there were six officers who held positions of importance and decided to remain behind. These included the former Kings School student, Captain Guy Manning, whose previous New Guinea experience saw him placed as Head of Native Affairs, and his brother, Captain Charles Manning, Judge of the Territory, who was staying until a replacement could be appointed. Lieutenant Collins remained as Officer in Charge of Native Police, Lieutenant Lyng as Government printer and interpreter whilst Lieutenant Gillam of the RAN Reserve became King's Harbourmaster at Rabaul. Major Heritage

Sgt. Bill Dovey (2nd left) and Native Police
AWM: P04117.001.1

continued as Military Secretary but the incoming Colonel Pethebridge regarded him as too valuable in the area of instruction and training and therefore of greater use to the AIF (2)

It is not the purpose here to examine in detail the proceedings that occurred during the period of military occupation. It is of interest to have a brief look at particular problems, especially those unusual administrative problems peculiar to the situation and environment in New Guinea and also to examine what life was like in general for the rank and file members of the occupying forces…

William Miller's involvement with affairs in New Guinea ended in December, 1914 when HMAS *Encounter* covered the landing at Madang. Apart from that there were a couple of minor but somewhat exciting episodes. In October, 1914, whilst patrolling in the Fiji-Samoan area, the *Encounter* captured the small German schooner, *Elfrede*. This episode went smoothly.

After being sent to Sydney for a re-fit, the *Encounter* was deployed on a series of voyages in the Pacific region, especially in the areas of Fiji and Samoa, in case any of the German squadron made a return.

In July, 1915 HMAS *Encounter* was sent to Fanning Island to land a garrison to protect the cable station there. The Germans had previously cut the Pacific cable and rumours were circulating that they would make another attempt. It was during this journey that the *Encounter* ran aground on Johnstone Island and had to put in at Hong Kong for repairs.

One of William Miller's ship-mates at this time was Boy First Class William Evan Allan who was to become Australia's last living veteran of active service during World War I. Given the age of William Allan and the fact that William Miller was an Officer's Steward it is likely that they were well acquainted as the former most probably performed cabin duties as part of his appointed tasks. (3)

The remaining months of William Miller's naval career were spent on patrol in the Fijian-Samoan region. As most of the Australian fleet was by now employed overseas it was left to *Encounter* and several cruisers of the Japanese Navy to patrol these waters and to act as escorts for convoys.

A highlight of his naval career came in February, 1916 when he was awarded the Good Conduct badge. He was also awarded 6 pounds, 13 shillings and 4 pence as prize money for war service. Early in March, 1916 he was on land-based placement at HMAS *Cerebus* prior to the termination of his Naval career on 20th March, 1916. (4)

Life for William Miller then proceeded on a different course. So too did life for those charged with the task of administering the former German New Guinea colonial possessions...

Group Portrait in the Officers' Mess
AWM: A03234

Administrative issues and unusual problems

The task facing Colonel Pethebridge and the Tropical Force was daunting. The area they were to administer was quite large with many scattered garrisons separated from Rabaul by either water or dense bush. They were to govern a large native population and, at times, a resentful German population. Yet the Garrison troops were themselves never large in number. The largest group was based at Rabaul and it consisted of three officers (one a medical officer), three N.C.O.'s, fifty-nine men and thirty-one, at times unpredictable, native police. By late February, 1915 troop numbers across the entire area of occupation totalled approximately 550-590 men. (5)

Native affairs and cannibalism

A wide variety of problems arose because much of the commercial activities in the occupied area relied heavily on the use of native labour. The New Guinea natives were well-accustomed to the tropical conditions and therefore constituted the best workforce. Few disagreed with this assessment but it was in matters of how and where the workers were recruited and how they were disciplined which required close supervision by the new administrators.

The initial approach was to continue to let matters operate as they had done under the previous German administration. However it soon became apparent that there were particular circumstances which had to be more closely supervised. The Australians were very mindful of where the German plantation owners travelled in order to recruit workers. There was always the possibility that, during boat trips to nearby islands in search of workers, the Germans may try to make contact with the German military authorities. They also had to ensure that the workers were enlisted willingly and not hijacked in the manner akin to the way in which Queensland sugar plantation owners had sometimes hijacked Kanaka labourers as workers during the nineteenth century.

Complicating matters for the new administration was the fact that the white population was vastly outnumbered by the native population and they could not always rely on the German plantation owners to co-operate. In addition, the new administrators had to be wary of any adverse side effects which might arise as the result of inter-tribal wars. One observer recorded his account of one such episode for the Adelaide paper, *The Chronicle:*

"An inter-tribal warfare broke out... the plantation workers came from everywhere, and there were arrows flying about at night a great deal thicker than was pleasant..." (6)

A further complicating factor... and one with which few in the administration had previous experience... was interference with happily-placed native workers by other, savage and more primitive New Guinea tribesmen. For example, a problem had arisen in Bougainville where the peaceful natives from the coastal areas were threatened by the savages of the inland tribes. These primitive tribes would conduct raids on the plantations, making off with the female workers and either killing, or sometimes capturing, and eating the male workers.

In October, 1915 the Administrator directed Captain H. Ogilvy[1]

1 Major H.L.S. Balfour Ogilvy, M.B.E., D.C.M., Auctioneer of Renmark, S.A., b.Castleton, Ireland, 3 April, 1876.

to pursue and punish some native chiefs guilty of just such an offence. One of those was a particularly nasty piece of work, a Chief by the name of Bowu. Ogilvy and his men found and surrounded the Chief's village. He decided to rush the village and in the ensuing melee Bowu was captured. He was identified by the native men in Ogilvy's party. Punishment was brutal and swift. Bowu was beheaded and the head was shown to the friendly chiefs who were extremely pleased to see that he was indeed dead... but the matter did not end there. A further three native chiefs were captured but not before Police-Master Jenkins[2] had to grapple with and throw to the ground Chief Lapapiri who was still clinging to his spears. (7)

According to the New Guinea natives themselves, it was only the old men who were cannibals. Nonetheless it was not a problem adequately dealt with in any administrative guide book made available to the occupying forces.

Occasionally native workers would run away from their employers, be pursued and subsequently subjected to corporal punishment. It is in this matter that the Australians made changes to the arrangements set in place by their German predecessors. It had been the practice of the German administration to issue licences to approved employers to inflict corporal punishment on their employees. In August 1915, the new Administration restricted the right to inflict corporal punishment to a Government official appointed as the result of a Judge's or a Court's decision.

At about the same time reforms were made to the laws governing the recruitment of native labourers making it more difficult to avoid being convicted for kidnapping them against their will. (8)

2 Lieutenant A. W.Jenkins, Hospital attendant of Sydney, b. Birmingham, England, May, 1884.

People and taxes

In general terms, the Australians continued the taxation system instituted by the Germans. Basically this consisted of a head-tax of between five to ten shillings levied on all males above the age of 12 who were not in the employment of a white man or the government. In return the natives received medicine and medical treatment, protection, facilities for trading and a means by which to settle their grievances. Of course problems arose in collecting these taxes but usually these were resolved by having those in debt work that debt off as labourers.

This system did have its advantages. The collectors had to maintain direct contact with the native population and were therefore able to report back on potential problems such as unrest or the emergence of major sickness issues.

It is interesting that, in some areas, significant problems arose due to an imbalance between the sexes within the population. The recruitment of labourers and also the illegal practice of "black-birding" (kidnapping) in New Ireland created an unusual situation. For years the youngest and fittest had been taken from the region resulting in a significant decline in the native population of that area. Females in this outpost were significantly outnumbered by males resulting in polyandry and a declining birthrate. Captain Guy Manning consulted with local missionaries and settlers before reporting to the Administrator that the natives were fast dying out and something needed to be done. As a result the decision was made in October, 1915 that no recruitment of workers would occur in New Ireland unless it was with the express approval of the Administrator. (9)

A storm in a teacup

There was another incident which did for a time cause some concern. In July, 1915 Acting Administrator Lieutenant-Colonel Toll received reports that a vessel by the name of *Maverick* had left San Francisco with arms onboard and was headed for the Dutch East Indies. He was concerned that it may stop off in New Guinea and communicate with Germans living there. Toll took all reports that he received very seriously and proceeded to intern some 93 Germans in Rabaul and a further 33 in Herbertshohe. He also declared martial law and detained all missionaries at their stations. Horses and vehicles were confiscated and patrols begun of the waters nearby.

Nothing more was heard of the *Maverick*. When Pethebridge returned to the area he decided that nothing had occurred which warranted the continuation of martial law. Whilst no evidence came to light that a plot had actually been conceived, it was decided that Toll had acted in an appropriate manner. There was no major arms cache as Toll had believed, although some isolated undeclared rifles, shotguns and revolvers had been found.

The spectre of distrust

Throughout the period of Australian administration those in authority were always dogged by a sense of distrust as to what the Germans were up to and how best to supervise their activities. It is true that there was a certain amount of resentment from within the German community that they were no longer in charge of affairs. In their moments of greatest paranoia, the leaders of the occupying forces feared that resentful Germans may have been guilty of fomenting disloyalty and rebellion among the native population. If such was to occur, the task of conducting government would have become quite dangerous, if not impossible, unless extensive reinforcements of troops were brought in.

There were times when the German plantation owners would lecture their native workers on how much better off they had been under their German masters and that, one day, those same masters would again be in control. However in reality, the possibility of insurrection as a result of such undermining of Australian authority was more imagined than real. It was far more advantageous to the German commercial interests if harmonious relations were kept in place. It was also safer that way, as an unchecked native uprising would most assuredly not stop to consider which language a particular white master spoke. On the issue of preserving a safe and tranquil society, the Germans had more to lose than gain by stirring up trouble.

In fact there were those at home in Australia who were critical of the fact that German commercial activities were allowed to continue at all. Such critics considered that these should have been handed over and placed under the control of the occupying forces. However, this view overlooked the fact that it was in the best interests of the new administrators for existing structures and practices to stay in place rather than usurp them, especially when the newcomers lacked experience in such matters. There was also the point that control under martial law was not the same as annexation; if New Guinea had been formally annexed then the legal and political situation would have been vastly different. In addition, it was noted that all exports from New Guinea now went to Australia; no longer was Germany the beneficiary.

Firearms, smugglers, women and pigs

Within the captured territory the natives had, for some considerable time, hunted the beautifully-plumed bird of paradise. Their feathers were highly prized and the plumage of a single bird could fetch from five to ten pounds on the European market. The new administrators were loathe to interfere with native hunting practices but they were also reluctant to allow them to have access to firearms. In addition the hunting of the bird of paradise was illegal in the neighbouring territory of Papua and so it was only a matter of time before they became a protected species in the former German colonial areas as well.

This goal was achieved in stages. A licence system, initiated by the Germans, was continued and later on it was decided that anyone in possession of three or more birds had to declare and register them. This did not stop the killing of these beautiful birds as it was too easy to disappear into the scrub on some other pretext and then smuggle the slain birds out through the Dutch territory. Some efforts were made to stop this illicit smuggling but the size of the occupied territory and the length of its coastlines made the task exceedingly difficult.

An important figure in the administrative structure was the District Officer, known as the "Kiap" and in the eyes of the natives a man of considerable stature. Much of his time was spent in exercising his functions with a close eye to native customs and interests. He could adjudicate on such matters as the maintenance of roads, the validity of a marriage or the granting of a divorce. A lot of his time was spent in settling disputes between natives:

"It has been ungallantly said that, in New Guinea, women and pigs are the bane of a natives's existence, and that three-fourths of a district officer's time is taken up in settling questions of disputed ownership of one or the other." (10)

There were many things said about the type of duties involved in administering the territories previously under the control of Germany. These duties were variously described as "challenging" or "arduous" or having to be performed under stifling conditions. Seldom was the word "boring" used in this context.

Chapter 15

GARRISON LIFE

"In three words I can sum up everything I have learned about Life. It goes on."

(Robert Frost)

"Boredom" was a word sometimes used when discussing the daily life of the men left behind to administer the former German possessions in New Guinea. Strangely enough, boredom also became a part of life for those in the trenches at the Western Front; the difference there being, this boredom was often punctuated by periods of sheer terror.

Obviously, the men who remained in New Guinea as part of the occupying forces were required to give up normal civilian life and freedoms; they were obliged to subject themselves to military discipline and the monotony of daily garrison life. Not for them was there the tumult of the battle zone; nor was there the opportunity to perform great deeds of courage. As the days and weeks rolled by with a great similarity their enthusiasm and interest tended to flag.

News from home

As was the case with most serving in war zones they longed for news from home or for news of how the war was going. Initially, only basic scraps of information were received by wireless. Later this was replaced by twice-weekly transmissions of a radiogram giving news from the war and major events in Australia. These transmissions were vetted by the censor. A transcript was then made available to all departments and also distributed to the various outstations.

"In this way the fortunes of political parties, the progress of recruiting, the dispatch of further contingents to France, the deeds of the AIF and even the winners of the Sydney and Melbourne cups were made known to the troops in New Guinea." (1)

Before distribution to the various outposts, these communiques were censored by the Administrator in case they contained information deemed unsuitable for passing on to the German residents.

It took as long as six weeks for mail to arrive from Australia but there were times when the delay could be as long as ten weeks.

News and propaganda

The German colonists were just as keen to receive news from outside even if they often regarded the news which filtered down to them as wartime propaganda. The natives were no doubt confused by the whole business, understanding little more than the fact that the British and Germans were fighting each other in some other place. From time to time the administrative officials would give a "good fellow" talk to the police boys, government labourers and house-servants during which they would tell them the British were winning the war and would never be leaving New Guinea.

Both the occupying Administration and the German residents were astute enough to realise that, being vastly outnumbered, it was in both their interests to exert firm control over the natives rather than stir up trouble. However there were occasions when certain German missionaries, behind the shield of their religious functions, assured the natives that Germany would again resume control. When the authorities became aware of this happening it was investigated and, where necessary, dealt with under the provisions of the War Precautions Act.

One such incident arose in Rabaul in June, 1916. A German planter had admitted telling his native labourers that when the Germans came back the natives would be made to "savee plenty"... punished severely. The Administrator was scathing in his condemnation of these comments. He pointed out that as well as fostering a dangerous situation they were a breach of the oath of neutrality taken by the planter. He published his comments in the *Government Gazette* as a warning to all residents.

Rogues gallery

With little to do it wasn't long before the less-disciplined among the AN&MEF contrived to create trouble by taking part in various illegal activities. As early as October, 1914 five Australian soldiers stole money, liquor and cigars from a Catholic mission near Rabaul. In

November a further robbery occurred and this time the victims were Chinese and the offenders were members of the military police. In the former robbery only one offender, an army private, was apprehended. He was dishonourably discharged and sentenced to three years gaol. Of the military policemen, two received a gaol sentence of four years whilst the other two were sent to gaol for three years.

By 13th November, 1914, just two months after hostilities had ceased some fifteen servicemen had been sentenced for offences such as robbery, receiving, forgery and refusal to obey orders.[1] Colonel Holmes despaired about the calibre of some of the men under his control. By 1915 there were reports of widespread looting appearing in the Australian press. The matter was raised in Parliament. The government was concerned that the good name of Australian troops would be badly damaged.

For Colonel Holmes these incidents of looting could not have occurred at a worse time. News reports concerning them were circulating in Australia at the same time as he returned from New Guinea. He was entitled to feel that his welcome home would be a warm one as he had achieved his assigned task. Whilst he personally did not prefer the role of administrator to that of military leader he gave every indication that he had also carried those duties out in an admirable manner. Yet despite all his achievements his homecoming, rather than be a time of widespread acclaim, tended to be clouded by these incidents of looting.

Attorney-General Billy Hughes was particularly concerned. The looting incidents in New Guinea were happening at about the same

1 Elsewhere it has been stated that from 12 September to 31 December, 1914, 137 Australians were court-martialled in Rabaul for looting and that their punishments totaled 324 days of "field punishment" and 453 days of "forfeited pay".**The Neglected War**, H. Hiery,(1995), p.282.

time that members of the AIF were being trained in Egypt prior to their dispatch to Gallipoli. Their exploits when on leave in Cairo did not always present Australian soldiers in a good light. Peter Weir subsequently highlighted their behaviour in his epic movie, *Gallipoli*. Hughes received reports of misdeeds in New Guinea just as he was dealing with the backlash from the flogging of the German miscreants mentioned earlier.

Some of the less scrupulous soldiers felt it was their right to simply steal from those they had conquered and that acquiring loot was quite acceptable. Apparently, they saw goods so acquired as the spoils of war. One Petty Officer reported to his aunt that he had so much loot it would take two strong men to carry it. A couple of soldiers thought nothing of stealing fowls and a pig from New Guinea natives in order to supplement their Christmas dinner in 1914.

Holmes' replacement, Colonel Pethebridge, also had to deal with the problem of looting. Even some officers were caught up as a result of their desire to acquire "souvenirs". Lieutenant-Colonel John Paton had been in charge of a force of soldiers and sailors who had captured the German vessel *Komet* in October, 1914. He souvenired a knife, fork and spoon from the ship and was also charged with stealing a beer mug, wine glasses, teapot and dinner service but these latter charges were later withdrawn due to lack of evidence. A court of inquiry set up in Australia to investigate the matter found that Paton had not acted with felonious intent and he was honourably acquitted. Similar charges against other officers were also dismissed. In general terms it was felt that acquisition of small items as souvenirs was acceptable; large scale accumulation of booty was not.

This particular incident was significant in two ways. Coming as it did, early in the period of administration, it exemplified the need to take greater precautions against looting. This was done; it was for this very reason that Pethebridge had incurred the wrath of the departing troops when he ordered that their luggage be subjected to inspection.

Billy Hughes was certainly not impressed with the reports of looting. But the impact of it upon Holmes' achievements was unfair to Holmes. He had acquitted himself well in achieving his appointed task; he was keen to push on and contribute to the war effort in Europe. Holmes did not need, nor did he welcome, this ending to his role in New Guinea. (2)

What do you do with a drunken sailor?

Colonel Holmes' son, Lieutenant Basil Holmes, had to deal with a case of drunken behaviour which could well have had serious consequences. He was on a former German steamer the *Mekong* heading from Rabaul to Kieta on Bougainville when he noticed that the ship's Captain was under the influence of liquor and steering the ship in a north-by-westerly course instead of heading south-east. When questioned, the Captain responded by talking wildly about reefs in the area. Holmes, who had done this trip before, stated he had been previously assured that the area was clear of reefs altogether.

Holmes became so concerned about the Captain's erratic behaviour that at 10am (22nd December, 1914) he relieved the Captain of control of the ship and at 11am he gave the First mate, Able Seaman Jackson,[2] control of the ship. Holmes interviewed him a number of

2 Commander J.M. Jackson,R.N., Commanded HMAS *Una*, 1914-16.

times over the next few hours and each time the deposed Captain pleaded with him not to make an adverse report. Upon arrival at Kieta, Holmes went ashore but when he returned to the vessel at 4pm that same day he found that the Captain was again under the influence of alcohol. By 7pm he was hopelessly drunk.

For the return journey the Captain was removed from his position and First Mate Jackson was again placed in charge of the ship. When the matter was brought before Colonel Holmes, the drunken mariner was relieved from duty, told to leave Rabaul and Colonel Holmes made a recommendation that his name be struck off the list of Royal Navy Reserve officers. (3)

Climate and environmental factors

Many of the letters written by members of the occupying forces to their friends and relatives at home make mention of the oppressive heat and humidity which continually sapped the strength of the letter writers. They also told of the beautiful birds, strange and exotic creatures and plants not familiar to those from sub-tropical regions.

It so happened that during the period of the military occupation New Guinea managed to stage some special events for the benefit of its new residents.

One such event was the severe earthquake which hit Rabaul on the night of 1st January, 1916. It was the most severe that had been witnessed there for some 5-17 years. Despite its severity no major structural damage occurred; this was attributed to the tremors having a rotary, rather than a vertical heaving motion. Another major earthquake which struck on 7th May 1919 caused much damage to property. The men were put to work effecting repairs. (4)

The sessions of heavy rain came to be welcomed as a relief from the oppressive humidity but few were ready for what would hit them in the closing days of 1915. From 27th December, 1915 until 13th January, 1916 rainfall at Rabaul amounted to 43 inches (1075 mm). (5)

These weather events were very trying but it was their impact on the health and well-being of the members of the occupying forces which was crucial. The consequences were often far more serious.

Death and disease

As the men of the occupying forces were new to the tropics they were not familiar with tropical diseases. Some of these diseases did in fact take their toll but the situation could well have been far worse had not measures been taken. The Medical officers worked tirelessly to do all that could be done to minimise the impact of diseases on the men under their supervision. They realised quite early in the piece that is was better for the Australian government to send to New Guinea only fit men aged under forty rather than send men considered too old or too unfit for combat duties in Europe.

Lieutenant-Colonel Howse, the Principal Medical Officer, devoted himself to the administrative side of the task, setting in place hospitals and adequate sanitation systems. He remained in New Guinea for only the first month but he had a very capable assistant in Captain F.A. Maguire. The measures they took proved effective. For example, under the previous German administration, 57% (or 76 out of 133) of all deaths which occurred in New Guinea, in the period 1886–1914, were as the result of malaria or blackwater fever. (6) Death as a result of these diseases continued under the occupying forces but not as drastically or in this proportion.

This was no doubt in large measure due to the efforts of the medical staff who did whatever they could to avoid the spread of disease. Time and again they advised the men to drink only water which had been sterilised. Quinine was used to combat malaria but it was found that it became much more effective once the men had become more acclimatised. Those in authority ensured that measures were taken to attack the breeding areas of the mosquito. Quinine parades were held every second day and sometimes every day during the rainy season. Mosquito nets were made available and the importance of using them was impressed on the men. The first *Government Gazette*, dated 15th October, 1914 stated:

"MOSQUITO NETS: These must be placed in position ready for sleeping at 5:45pm daily, and inspected by an officer from each company." (7)

The medical officers had to battle with a wide variety of diseases. These included malaria, dysentery, pneumonia, blackwater fever. In addition there were seriously uncomfortable but seldom fatal skin conditions such as ringworm, sycosis, prickly heat (caused by excessive perspiration) and dhobi itch.

Blackwater fever was a complication of a malarial infection often caused by an unfavourable interaction of the malaria parasite and quinine. Private Joseph Read was one unfortunate who succumbed as a result of blackwater fever. Born in England he had enlisted at Adelaide one month after Rabaul had been taken. He was a plasterer at the time but had previously spent seven years in the Dorset regiment. He was only three months in New Guinea when he died at Kieta on Bougainville Island. In a poignant footnote, his personal effects were sold for 3 pounds and ten shillings. As late as May 1920 his brother, Arthur, was still trying to ascertain where his effects ended up. (8)

Another man who died under unfortunate circumstances was Private Arthur John Lindsay. He had worked as a miner until December, 1917 when he enlisted at the age of 34. After having been sent with the AIF to Britain in the last months of the war he had been almost immediately returned home due to defective vision. Having been deemed unfit for combat duty he was subsequently sent to Rabaul to assist with the surveying of roads. Sometime later he was sent onto Madang where he fell ill on 16th June, 1919 with double pneumonia. He died the next day. (9)

The men of the occupying force were fortunate in that they managed to avoid some complaints which were an issue for the New Guinea natives. These included elephantiasis, hook-worm, cus-cus and tropical ulcers.

Things began to improve, there were only six deaths due to malaria in 1915 and after this time there were no more serious outbreaks. One of the six deaths due to malaria in 1915 was Private James Morgan. He had spent over 7 years in the Royal Navy followed by fifteen years in the Victorian Navy. After joining the AN&MEF he was sent to the isolated area of Marienberg on the Sepik River which is where he died of malaria on 19th January,1915. His wife, Margaret did not hear of his death until well over one month later. She was later awarded a war pension of 52 pounds per annum. (10)

Regimented lifestyle

As to be expected for members of the military, the day-to-day activities of the men of the occupying forces was highly regimented. The very first *Government Gazette* listed an extensive array of regulations which covered everything from the moment they were awoken by *Reveille*. Each man had to carry 50 rounds of ammunition at all times, Chinatown was off-limits, no alcohol could be purchased in bottles, alcoholic drinks were limited to two per day and so on. Special regulations (aimed at fighting diseases) also existed…no fruit was allowed in the barracks unless in a mosquito-proof receptacle; tinned food had to be eaten as soon as it was opened; regular inspections were made of the latrines. (11)

Unfortunately, the men did not always follow these regulations to the letter and sometimes the consequences were disastrous. On 7th October, 1914 some men foolishly handled some signal rockets which exploded causing serious injury to Private G. James, who was some distance away at the time, and Private W. Guard, both of "A" Coy.

Both men were treated by Dr. Wicks before being sent to hospital at Namanula where they made a full recovery. (12)

Private William Guard could well have been advised to buy Lottery tickets (not that they existed back then in New Guinea) as he was similarly lucky on three further occasions. After returning to Australia he enlisted in the AIF and was dispatched to Gallipoli. Here he received a shrapnel wound to the head and was evacuated to Egypt. By mid-1916 he found himself in France near the town of Pozieres, just in time to take part in the Battle of the Somme. On 4th August, 1916 he was involved in a successful attack upon some German trenches.

He was then sent to a post forward of the lines, but left his coat and pack behind in the trenches. Again he was wounded but was able to return to the trench, bringing with him another wounded man. When he checked his belongings he found that a bullet had penetrated his notebook which was in his coat pocket but which he, fortunately, had not been wearing at the time.

In November, 1916, the now Lieutenant Guard, was again wounded. Ultimately he managed to survive all his wounds, returned to Australia and settled in the Queenbeyan and Canberra region. In 1936 he donated the damaged pocketbook to the Australian War Memorial. (13)

Accidental deaths

As was the case when Germany was in control some deaths occurred due to accidents. In some cases this was the result of the victim not exercising due care; at other times the surrounding environment was a contributing factor.

Quite early in the period of the new administration there was an accident caused by carelessness. On 14th October, 1914 Albert Martin Wates died as a result of his rifle discharging whilst he was cleaning it in the Rabaul barracks. That is not the full story. Wates had been unaware that his rifle still had a bullet in it when he reached up to take it off its peg. The rifle discharged, wounding him in the upper left leg. Privates Hall and Hunter were near-by and immediately applied a tourniquet. Soon afterwards he was attended by Doctor Maguire. Subsequently, a decision was made to amputate the leg. According to the Court of

Inquiry, Wates survived the surgery but succumbed to shock associated with the trauma. He was 27 years and 4 months of age.

In fact the story of Wates' life is quite a sad one in itself. Born in 1887 he had previously spent two-and-a-half years in the Scottish Rifles before enlisting in the AN&MEF. As a child he lost his father at the age of four and his mother a year later. In the months after his death, a Mrs M. Phillips wrote to the military authorities stating, that although she was not a blood relative, she was about as close as possible to being a mother to Albert Wates as anyone could be. She therefore asked that parcels which she had sent to him be passed on to his good friend, Arthur Kearns.

In 1920 his eldest sister, Mrs Harvey, asked if she could be given his War medals. Wates may not have been mourned by a mother, but he was mourned nonetheless. (14)

A member of the first AN&MEF expeditionary force who remained behind to perform an important administrative role, also died as the result of an accident. As mentioned earlier, Captain Guy Manning had elected to remain in New Guinea after the departure of Colonel Holmes. His knowledge of the area and previous experience as a plantation manager were deemed invaluable and so he was duly appointed to the District Office in New Ireland as Officer-in-Charge at Kawieng. He was killed after being thrown from his motorcycle whilst performing his duties, three miles from Kawieng at about 4:30pm on 18th June, 1915.

A Court of Inquiry was held on 23rd-24th June, 1915 and the presiding Judge was Major Seaforth MacKenzie who later wrote the Official War History of the New Guinea campaign under the guidance of C.E.W. Bean. Two soldiers gave evidence as well as a native whose testimony was given verbally in pidgin and written down by another soldier. Guy's wife, Lynda, testified that he was temperate in his habits and on the day of his death he had been fit, healthy and happy.

Guy Manning had been a devoted father and during the early part of his appointment he wrote many poignant letters to his wife, Lynda. She later travelled to New Guinea and lived with him at Kawieng. Soon after the inquiry she and their daughter, Mary, returned to Sydney, later residing at Bowral, NSW. (15)

Guy Manning with his daughter Mary
Courtesy of The King's School, Parramatta

Rest and relaxation

Quite early in the period of administration there was the realisation that there was a need to provide some form of recreational activities to maintain morale and to break down the tedium of a regimented lifestyle for those living far from home. Even that was to be well organised rather than spontaneous. The first issue of the *Government Gazette* stated that:

"All amusements, sports and entertainments will be subject to the control of the Committee appointed by the OC the garrison." (16)

Measures were made to establish recreational pursuits. Rifle shooting was a popular pastime so rifle ranges were set up at Rabaul and near Matupi. In Rabaul a tennis court was established and a cricket pitch laid down. Swimming was catered for by netting off an area in Simpson Harbour, safe from stingrays and sharks. Arrangements were even made for films to be sent up from Australia and picture shows were given from time to time. Occasionally, officers were able to take a cruise to the islands around Rabaul. They had at their disposal horses for riding and some officers even had cars.

The occasional game of Australian Rules football was held despite the often oppressive heat and humidity. One such game, played in October:

"... took place between South Australian and Victorian teams. The game resulted in South Australia scoring 6 goals and 13 behinds to Victoria's 3 goals and 15 behinds. The winners seemed to be able to do anything with the ball, and gave their opponents a lively time of it." (17)

In the outlying stations fewer facilities such as those mentioned above existed and so the officers there were more likely restricted to

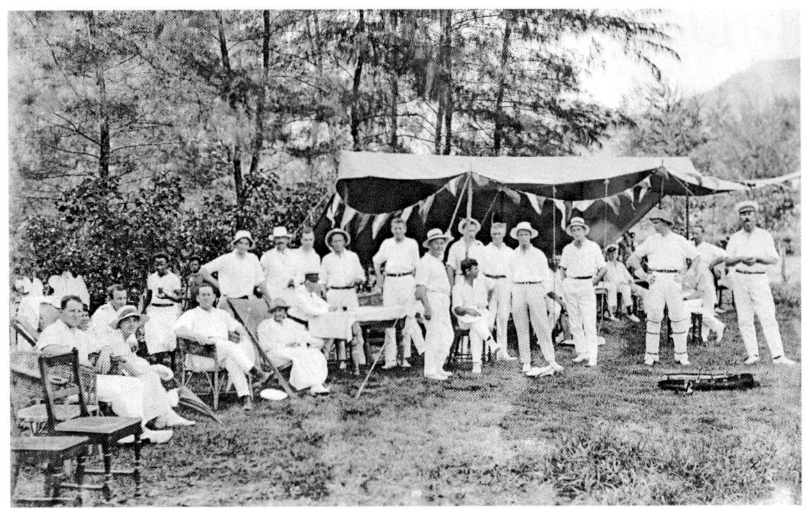

Cricket Match, Rabaul 1916
AWM: J03138

excursions into the nearby bush. Recreational facilities for the unpromoted were considerably more limited.

Most social life centred around the "wet" canteen. This became a favourite gathering place where the men met to play cards, draughts, billiards, chess or simply to read. Suitable reading material was difficult to attain. Some members of the Chinese community were able to provide a welcome alternative to the food provided by the Garrison kitchen. In Rabaul a store was converted into what became a popular restaurant.

Of course things were somewhat different for the officers. They set aside rooms in the former German administrative buildings which were set up almost in the manner of gentlemen's clubs; places where they could meet informally and discuss events over a port and a cigar before being served their meals by trusted and trained natives. These facilities were not widespread and generally were restricted to the larger areas such as Rabaul. Administrative officers in the more isolated outposts had to rely more on their own initiative and were only able to mingle with a considerably smaller number of fellow officers.

Newspapers

There were some in the force who had journalistic experience and so it was inevitable that sooner or later a local newspaper would appear. One such publication was a two page news-sheet known as *The Namanula Times* which first appeared in December, 1915. This paper only ever produced two editions and was later replaced by a monthly newspaper called *The Rabaul Record*. This paper ended in the middle of 1918.

In Christmas 1918 another publication appeared called *Passed by Censor*. This publication was also destined for a short lifespan. It began with an extensive account of the military campaign which had occurred back in 1914 and then went on to present various offerings from members of the occupying forces. One section, titled *Whizbangs* used humour to reveal details of their life in New Guinea. A so-called "For Exchange" item offered:

"WANTED to EXCHANGE: Iceworks, in good condition; guaranteed to work 2 days a month, and can be used alternatively as a bath heater, for motor cycle or tin of Capstans."

Gunner, perhaps with aspirations for entering the world of Real Estate Sales made the following offering:

"VACANT ALLOTMENT NEAR MATUPI; not required by previous tenants. Beach frontage, splendid view, close tram and train, swimming, boating, fishing, earthquakes, mosquito-hunting."

Reading these "classifieds" reveals that the men were well aware of the changes that the Armistice would bring to their lives and were looking forward to them with anticipation:

"Vast quantities of war material will have to be disposed of when the time comes for demobilisation. It is understood that OC Public Works has already requisitioned for a few tanks". (18)

One humorous item also had a serious undertone when it hinted at the fact that many new arrivals from Australia were promptly rejected by the medical board and sent back home.

"Koko-po for the Air. The Health Resort of the Pacific. Cricket , Golf, Physical Jerks. Vacancies for a few more boarders." (19)

While Colonel Holmes was acting as Administrator he became concerned about the maintenance of the botanic gardens established at Rabaul by his German predecessors. Initially, the gardens had been looked after by Private J. Gibb (formerly of Neutral Bay) but Holmes arranged with the Defence Department for a Howard Newport to be sent up from the experimental gardens in Cairns, Queensland. Colonel Pethebridge also saw the relevance of the gardens to the agricultural interests of New Guinea but he directed that they also be used as a place for growing vegetables and fruit for consumption by the garrison as a means of combating diseases such as beri beri. (20)

During 1916 the Rabaul Garrison band was formed. It was led by an experienced bandmaster, Sergeant-Major M. C. Nuttall. Instruments were donated by such organisations as the Victoria Racing Club. (21) This band was still providing music for entertainment and marches right through to the end of the war.

From time to time concerts were organised to provide some variety and diversion for the men. One such concert was held at

Rabaul on 21st April, 1915. The program included songs such as *The Galloping Major, All's Well, Dear Old Home* and *Ring down the Curtain.* Corporal Court provided a humorous recitation and a group of men put together a sketch entitled *A lively day Recruiting.* (22)

A sense of adventure was needed for many who took part in these performances because few would have had previous acting experience. "Versatility" would also have been a key attribute as all parts, male and female, were to be played by the men. The audience too had to contribute; it needed to provide laughter and applause where appropriate and a "willing suspension of disbelief" for the more serious pieces.

In providing these musical and dramatic interludes the men of the occupying forces in New Guinea were no different to their countrymen in the other theatres of war. Nor were they any different from men in later wars, such as the prisoners working on the Burma-Siam railway. These performances were designed to maintain morale and to relieve boredom.

They were trying to comfort themselves with memories from home. They were also trying to maintain their sanity by reminding themselves that, eventually one day, life would return to normal.

Chapter 16

WHAT BECAME OF... ?

"It's choice-not chance-
that determines your destiny."

(Jean Nidetch)

The hostilities of mid-September, 1914 may have been short-lived but they had far-reaching consequences. For the first time, the new nation of Australia was introduced to the responsibilities associated with administering a territory outside its own national borders. These responsibilities were taken seriously by successive Australian governments. Australia's involvement with New Guinea was to continue for decades beyond that day; a day, when in the early weeks of World War I, six men lost their lives whilst displacing Germany from its wireless stations and colonial possessions in the Pacific region.

This brief military campaign had significant repercussions, on an individual level, for those who took part. For some of these men their life was changed forever and in a manner they had not anticipated. Some used their experiences as a spur to further contribute to the war effort. For many, the outcome was just the same as it was for almost all of those Australians who fought in the Great War; few saw their experiences as occasions for achievement of personal glory. They were to remember most the horror and the waste of life. Above all they clung to the mateship.

When looking over the subsequent careers of the military leaders of the New Guinea campaign it is quite astounding just how many of them went on to illustrious careers, either as part of the military or in civilian life or both.

The subsequent stories of minor participants in the New Guinea hostilities are also of interest.

What became of William Miller, the Officer's Steward after he returned to Sydney on HMAS *Encounter*?

William MILLER (1886-1960)

As well as receiving a Good Conduct badge just before the end of his term with the Navy, William Miller received the amount of 6 pounds, 13 shillings and 4 pence as prize money for war service. This payment, an old naval tradition, helped tide him over as he made up his mind about what to do next.

He stayed with his parents during the next few months, often recalling for either them, or his friends, his exploits onboard HMAS *Encounter*.

"We got to fire the big guns and didn't the Hun sit up and take notice..." or "When we went to Madang they weren't so brave then..."

Miller also brought back from the Pacific islands some souvenirs such as unusual but colourful paintings of peaceful beaches. These were much appreciated and remain within the family even today. He spent many hours talking with his mates over a beer and it was during such occasions that two things happened which were to impact on his future.

After a few ales one evening he and some friends attended a nearby dance. It was here that he met Ada Perry who had come to Sydney from Orange to visit friends. William Miller was quite impressed with the perky personality of Ada and decided that he would keep in touch with her. It was also whilst enjoying the company of his mates that he realised that so many of the men from the AN&MEF, having been discharged, simply re-enlisted in the Australan Imperial Forces and were undergoing further training.

So, on 16th September, 1916, almost two years to the day after the landing at Kabakaul, William Miller enlisted in the AIF It was recorded that he had a tattoo, "Death before Dishonour" on his upper right arm; yet another naval tradition. He was appointed to A Coy depot Battalion as a Private and two months later he embarked with the 7/60 Battalion onboard the *Afric* bound for Plymouth. In March, 1917 he was sent to Westham for instruction as a cook and from there he was despatched to France, bound for the battlefields of the Western Front.

Fate decreed that William Miller was not destined for battle. In July, 1917 he was admitted to hospital suffering from severe pain in the abdominal region. Apparently a badly-performed appendix procedure he had undergone back in 1908 had come back to haunt him. After spending some time in hospital he was classified as unfit for military service and returned to Australia per A68 *Anchises* in November, 1917, disembarking at Melbourne.

William Miller made his way back to Sydney, motivated not just by the need to live with his parents but also with a desire to again meet up with Ada Perry. Eventually he was able to gain work once more with the NSW Railways. The rail system was also the means by which he travelled to Orange to catch up with Ada and to meet her family. Their courtship initially involved a number of trips to Orange until the day he finally summoned the courage to propose.

Ada Perry became Mrs William Miller on 2nd October, 1918, just under six weeks before the end of the Great War. Two months later William applied for and was denied a war pension on the grounds that "the member's incapacity was not greater than at enlistment". He was, however, awarded the 1914/15 Star, the British War Medal and the Victory Medal.

Ada Miller proved to be an excellent cook and sometimes worked as a cook at hotels and restaurants near where they lived in Merrylands. He continued to work on the railways and together they raised a family of four, beginning with the eldest, Charles who was followed by his three sisters, Barbara, Gwennie and Winifred. Over the following years the family moved to Earlwood and lived there as the children themselves grew up and left home. In June 1948, the English-born, Ada, died at the age of 58. William remained in Earlwood still working on the railways but becoming increasingly morose. In time he met Alice Walton who he married in 1953 but this was destined to be a relatively short marriage as William Miller died in 1960 at the age of 74.

William Miller was somewhat unique in the sense that he twice went to war but never went into the thick of battle. He was certainly different from most of his comrades as he served in two different branches of the armed forces and both times as a volunteer. (1)

A story of twists and turns: Conrad Constantine Eitel.

Life for Conrad Eitel took a series of rather unusual turns. Few people are aware of his story; nor were many of his companions aware that he was a man of some achievement before he joined the AN&MEF.

To the officers of the AN&MEF Conrad Eitel, the former Sydney journalist, had proved of service during the advance up the road to Bitapaka because his ability to speak German fluently meant that he was called upon as an interpreter after the death of the English-speaking German, Sergeant Ritter.

Born of an English mother and a German father, Eitel had previously gained some renown as the Secretary for Sir Douglas Mawson's highly successful Antarctic Expedition. This was basically a fund-raising role which he occupied for a period of 18 months. Eitel lived in Germany until about the age of about eight or nine. In view of subsequent events it is significant to realise that his father, although born in Germany, had been a naturalised British subject for 52 years and had served for 35 years as a British government official, including the post of first private secretary to the Governor of Hong Kong.

Conrad Eitel had been a journalist in Hong Kong before moving to Sydney and then enlisting in the AN&MEF. He performed his role as interpreter admirably but was disliked by the Germans who saw him as a traitor. He returned to Sydney with the main group of the Expeditionary Force and was honourably discharged on 4th March, 1915.

As was the case with many of his comrades he decided to re-enlist and offer his services to the AIF. However he reasoned that they would not accept him because of his German background. So Conrad Eitel decided to enlist under the name of Lionel Lambert Easton; "Easton" was his mother's maiden name. At one stage he was based at Liverpool Army camp and was involved in the training program there.

However matters began to unravel for Eitel/Easton in December 1915. His true identity was discovered and court martial proceedings were instituted against him. The charge centred on the answer he gave to the question "Have you stated the whole, if any of your previous service?" In order to conceal his true identity he had lied by answering, "No". At least two of his superior officers testified in his favour; Captain William Sara stated that Eitel was "the finest soldier both from an administrative point of view and a drill point of view". Eitel's wife of fourteen years stated that he had not been outside Australia in the eighteen years that she had known him apart from his terms of involvement with the Mawson and New Guinea expeditions.

Evidence against him included unproven assertions that he was a German spy; there were suggestions that one of his accusers was the New Zealand Prime Minister. Lieutenant-Colonel Francis Heritage testified that whilst in New Guinea Eitel had told him that he had been in the German army as a reservist and that he had deserted. He also said that Eitel was not popular with some of the Naval personnel in New Guinea but that this was not unusual as there had been some animosity between the soldiers and the sailors of the AN&MEF. Finally, Heritage gave evidence that Eitel had done his job well.

Ultimately Conrad Eitel was found guilty as charged but with a recommendation for mercy on the grounds that he had committed the offence as the result of a desire to perform further active service. He was to be detained for 30 days and then discharged from the Army. Upon appeal the length of the term was reduced to 15 days of which he served about two before being discharged from the Army. Despite this he too was awarded the 1914/15 Star, the British War Medal and the Victory Medal. (2)

In their (adopted) country's service.

As mentioned in an earlier chapter 71% of the returning first expeditionary force enlisted in the AIF soon after their return. All of them did so with fervour and anticipation of the adventures ahead. But the outcome was vastly different from their expectations; often the outcome for one individual was quite dissimilar from that of his comrades in arms. It is interesting to have a brief look at the wartime careers of two men, both of whom played a role in the New Guinea hostilities.

Gerald Ashby HILL (1880-1931)

Lieutenant Hill played a significant role during the advance up the Bitapaka Road. Not initially intended as a leader of this advance he twice had leadership thrust upon him; after the wounding of Bowen and again after the death of Elwell. Gerald Hill was born in Birmingham, England on 1st May, 1880. He later became a Master Mariner and was loaned to the Australian Navy, coming out to Australia in 1913 onboard HMAS *Australia.* He went to New Guinea onboard HMAS *Yarra.*

During his time in New Guinea Hill kept a journal in which he wrote of his experiences in great detail and with considerable humour. A copy of this journal can be found in the Australian War Memorial He commented not only on the military activities but also the local flora and fauna and the indigenous population. In the late 1920s he donated to the National Museum a menu from a luncheon, hosted by the Millionaires Club of NSW, which had been signed by all four airmen on the first ever flight across the Pacific Ocean.

He was mentioned in despatches for his role in the New Guinea conflict. His war service included placements onboard HMAS *Yarra* and

HMAS *Torrens* as well as service in Malaysia and the Mediterranean. Like William Miller, he too was awarded Naval Prize money. His final promotion was to the rank of Lieutenant-Commander. In March, 1915 he married Marianne Wilson of Coogee, NSW and the couple were blessed with the arrival of a son in June 1916. He transferred to the retired list in July, 1920 and died on 4th May, 1931. His wife lived on in their Coogee home and died in September, 1970, aged 91. (3)

James Logie HARCUS (1881-1915)

Captain Harcus also played a role in the advance to Bitapaka and, like Gerald Hill, he too was serving across the other side of the world from his birthplace. James Harcus was born in Scotland on 22nd November, 1881, beginning his military career in 1899. From 1904-1907 he was in the Royal Scots Regiment and later in the Scottish Rifles. Harcus was a man of considerable talent and by the start of war he had been promoted to the rank of Captain and was also a qualified Barrister at Law.

He returned to Australia with the first expeditionary force and in May, 1915 he enlisted in the AIF. Subsequently he was sent to Gallipoli and in June, 1915 Harcus was promoted to the rank of Major. During October of that same year he spent three weeks in hospital suffering from dysentery.

Sadly, Major Harcus was killed in action on or about 11th December, 1915. He would have been one of the last fatalities in that theatre of the war. He had never married and his family were told that the exact location of his burial spot was unknown. His personal effects were listed as his wash kit, some photos, a ring and bank receipts. There was no diary. He was aged 34. (4)

Thomas Arthur BOND: Our First bravery award recipient.

As was the case with William Miller, Thomas Arthur Bond served with both the Naval forces and later enlisted in the AIF. He too was born in England (Bishops Waltham, Hants) but was working as an accountant in Brisbane at the time of his first enlistment.

Bond's citation for the DSO earned for his actions on the Bitapaka Road mentions "coolness under fire" and "showed great daring" when he quickly disarmed eight Germans. These attributes could well have been an outcome of his maturity because, at the time of that battle, he was almost fifty years old. Nor were these qualities isolated. He was to show his coolness and initiative on a number of occasions.

Thomas served as a Sub-Lieutenant and then Lieutenant in New Guinea, earning the DSO before returning home with the Expeditionary force and enlisting in the AIF In February, 1915 the decision was made to establish the Royal Australian Naval Bridging Train (RANBT) under the command of Lieutenant Bracegirdle. Thomas Bond was chosen as second in command, again with the rank of Lieutenant. Later that same year the RANBT headed for Gallipoli and in December, 1915 Bond was mentioned in despatches for his gallant behaviour. The RANBT was given a special commendation for the role it played during the successful evacuation from Gallipoli. From there the RANBT was sent to the Suez area in Egypt and in March, 1916 Bond was seconded to the Royal Navy. He was again mentioned in despatches in Cairo in August of that same year. At some stage he received a gunshot wound in the upper left forearm and that may have been the reason for his attachment to Australian headquarters for administrative purposes, in February,

1917. He was posted for duty to HMS *Hannibal* and from July, 1917 he temporarily filled the rank of Lieutenant-Commander in Egypt. Bond did not return to Australia until late 1919. He disembarked at Brisbane on 14th January, 1920 and later that same year his appointment with the AIF was terminated. Commander Bond applied for and was awarded the "Volunteer Officer's Decoration" (V.D.).

This man brought back from the war a well-earned reputation for bravery and resourcefulness but he also brought back the ongoing pain of a war wound. He received treatment for it during 1920 until finally it was decided that he was "unfit for general service" but "fit to work or vocational training". He was aged 60. (5)

The Sydney University men

Within this chapter there is a photograph of fifteen men, all of whom were graduates of Sydney University. The picture was taken in September, 1914, onboard HMAS *Berrima*. The picture was taken before hostilities began as one of the men in it is Captain Brian Pockley. In fact that photograph was lent to C.E.W. Bean by Captain Pockley's father, Dr. Francis Pockley.

What is remarkable about this picture is the fact that at least three of these men went on to distinguished careers after the war. Their careers were not directly related to the role they played in New Guinea but they were eminent enough to gain a mention in the Australian Dictionary of Biography or a similar publication.

Sydney University men onboard HMAS *Berrima* Sept. 1914
Back, (L-R): Pte.G.M. Edwards, Sgt. W. Dovey, Crp. J.S.Millner, Pte L.H. Lehmair.
Centre, (L-R): Crp. C.T. Collier, Ptes. H.L. Henley, J.B. Lane, F.E. Sandford, J.K. Henderson, Lt. C.E. Manning.
Front, (L-R): Capts. F.A.Maguire, B.C.A. Pockley, A.W. Ralston, Major R.H. Beardsmore, Capt. J.E. Donaldson.

Courtesy of the Pockley family; Official History WWI, C.E.W.Bean

Robert Henry BEARDSMORE (1873-1959)

After serving in New Guinea Robert Beardsmore served in Egypt and the Western Front where he was awarded the DSO and also mentioned in despatches. He was promoted to Lieutenant-Colonel but ended the war in an administrative role due to health issues.

After the war he became an accountant with the Department of Lands and was later involved with the 1929 miners strike at the Rothbury colliery. By refusing NSW Premier Lang's directive to pay all revenues into the State treasury he precipitated the chain of events which led to Lang's dismissal as Premier in the 1930s. Later resigning from this position, he served a lengthy term as treasurer of the Australian Jockey Club. He was also a member of the State Superannuation Board. In 1938 he was appointed M.B.E. (6)

Wilfred Robert (Bill) DOVEY (1894-1969)

Dovey achieved the rank of Sergeant in New Guinea and upon return to Australia he took up a teaching career and studied law at the University of Queensland. Bill Dovey was a tall man with a rich voice, an extensive vocabulary and his use of a monocle meant he was an imposing figure. Moving to NSW he was involved in many high profile legal cases, royal commissions and inquiries. He too, was a member of the committee of the Australian Jockey Club and served as an alderman of Waverley Council. In 1953 he was appointed as a judge to the Supreme Court of NSW. He was later criticised by State politicians for allegedly attending to his AJC business to the detriment of his judicial duties.

He and his wife, had two children. Their son, William, later became a judge on the family Court; their daughter married Edward Gough Whitlam, later to become Prime Minister of Australia. (7)

Frederick Arthur MAGUIRE (1888-1953)

Whilst in New Guinea Maguire worked tirelessly to combat the tropical diseases which threatened the lives of the men in his care. He firmly believed in preventative measures such as those designed to reduce breeding grounds for mosquitoes. He later served in a similar capacity on the Western front.

After the war he became a Master of Surgery and took on various teaching positions and consultative roles at Sydney University and Prince Alfred hospital. He specialised in Gynaecology. He was a Founding member of the Australian Regional Council of Obstetricians and Gynaecologists. From 1935-1939 he was Honorary surgeon to the Governor-General. (8)

All three of these men were high achievers and this brief summary hardly does them justice. Nor were they the only ones in the Sydney University picture worthy of mention. Charles Edye Manning, as mentioned earlier, remained behind in New Guinea to assist Colonel Pethebridge. Upon returning to Australia he was promoted to Captain and left for Egypt with the A.I.F. in May 1915. He was wounded at Gallipoli and promoted to the rank of Major. Later he was sent to the Western Front with the 24th Battalion where he was killed in action on 7th August,1916.

As mentioned in an earlier chapter, Charles' brother, Guy, also remained behind in New Guinea after the departure of the AN&MEF but was killed in a motorbike accident in 1915. Emily Manning, mother of Charles and Guy, thus lost two sons during the Great War. She was not the only mother in this account to do so. Helen Pockley and her husband, Francis, also lost two sons during this time. In addition to Brian's death in New Guinea in 1914, they lost their youngest son, John Graham Antill Pockley on the Western Front in 1918. The deaths of the Manning brothers and Charles Elwell meant that The Kings School had lost at least three of its former pupils who had later enlisted with the AN&MEF. (9)

Finally, among the other men in that Pockley family photograph were Captain J. E. Donaldson and Lieutenant-Colonel W. Ralston. The former was a medical practitioner from Vaucluse who had served in

New Guinea as a medical officer but who later went to the Western Front as a combatant where he died as the result of illness in August, 1916. (10)

Lieutenant-Colonel Ralston, CMG, having served with distinction, was awarded the DSO and went on to command the 20th Battalion AIF (1916/18) and later a Machine Gun Battalion (1918/19). (11)

Careers of distinction:

At least six other men involved with the AN&MEF have rated mentions in the Australian Dictionary of Biography. Of these six, only two had careers which were entirely within the military; one of those two had his life cut short in rather sad circumstances. Three of the six men remained behind in New Guinea, even if only for a short time, after the departure of the AN&MEF.

William HOLMES (1862-1917)

When Holmes returned to Australia with the first expeditionary force he, at times, felt that his achievements were undervalued because of scandals which had broken out involving looting. Despite his misgivings he was given command of the 5th Brigade and the rank of Brigadier General. He and his men landed in Gallipoli in August 1915 and during the evacuation which began in December of that year, Holmes was given command of the 2nd Division whose men were among the last to leave those shores. From Gallipoli he went to the Western front where he was involved in the fighting at Pozieres and Flers. He was later promoted to Major General and Commander of the 4th Division, only the third- citizen soldier to be given a divisional command. For his efforts he was mentioned in despatches four times and was also involved in other major battles such as Messines. He had been appointed CMG and also awarded the Russian Order of St. Anne. His luck ran out on 2nd July, 1917 whilst he was escorting the NSW Premier, W.A. Holman, around the battlefield. He was struck by a stray shell and died on the way to a field hospital. (12)

Sir Reginald Neville HOWSE (1863-1930)

Howse had already distinguished himself during the Boer War by rescuing a wounded man whilst under heavy enemy fire. This action gained him the Victoria Cross. He was taken prisoner during that war but released soon afterwards as he was a non-combatant. He was the Principal Medical Officer for the AN&MEF but only spent a little over a month in New Guinea. During that time he set up the basic infrastructure for the hospitals and sanitation systems. He returned to Australia, keen to join the AIF and was sent to Gallipoli where he established the ANZAC Medical Society. He was later posted to London and controlled Australian Army Medical services in Egypt and Palestine. He was involved in France and introduced surgical teams in the field.

His return to a private practice after the war was short-lived as he soon found himself again involved with Army Medical services and was chosen as one of the Australian delegates to the League of Nations. He later entered Federal parliament and had a variety of portfolios as a Minister; at different times these were Defence, Health, Repatriation and Home and Territories. He died of cancer in 1930. (13)

Roland Griffiths BOWEN (1879-1965)

Bowen distinguished himself with his, at times, unorthodox leadership on the road to Bitapaka. At all times he had been concerned for the welfare of his men and in return he himself was wounded. Soon after his return to Australia, his wife Margaret, died. He became the first State president of the returned Sailors' and Soldiers' Imperial league of Australia. Maintaining his involvement with Naval affairs, he was promoted to Commander in 1919 and later served as District Naval Officer in both Tasmania and Western Australia during the years 1919 to 1935. After retiring in 1936 he moved to Sydney. He was heavily involved with the St. John's Ambulance Association for a number of years and was appointed O.B.E. in 1957. (14)

Francis Bede HERITAGE (1877-1934)

After the men of the first expeditionary force returned to Australia, Heritage remained behind for a time as Deputy Administrator. He returned to Australia in mid-1915, was married to Rita Hill in October and promoted to Lieutenant-Colonel in December. His main area of expertise was military training and during 1916 he was Director of Training at Army HQ in Melbourne. He saw active service on the Western front during 1917 but was evacuated home in September of that year with rheumatic fever.

After the war he retained his involvement with the Army and especially with the training of troops. In August, 1922 he was appointed Commandant of the Royal Military College of Duntroon. This proved to be a difficult appointment as there was much pressure to disband the college. His work during this period saw his appointment as C.B.E.

in 1924. In 1929 he transferred to Sydney to command the 2nd Military district. Two years later he found himself again in control of the Royal Military College when it was down-sized and moved to Sydney. He was operated on for acute appendicitis in 1934 but died of peritonitis. At the time of his death there was an expectation that he had been about to be appointed Chief of the General Staff. (15)

Jens Sorensen LYNG (1868-1941)

Jens Lyng was born in Denmark and a devout Lutheran who migrated to Australia in 1891. In New Guinea he sometimes acted as an interpreter for Colonel Holmes but his main area of expertise was as a printer. Soon after the German capitulation he took over the Government Printing Office in Rabaul where he printed a fortnightly *Government Gazette* and a monthly paper, *The Rabaul Record*. He was also placed in charge of the censorship of letters written to the German planters. Promoted to Captain in 1916 he was placed as District Officer at Madang in 1918. Upon his return to Australia in September 1918 he was again given a role as censor of foreign mail and then in 1920 he transferred to the Bureau of Census and Statistics. Throughout the 1920s he did much to promote Danish migration to Australia. He was later transferred in his job to Canberra where he was promoted to librarian and draughtsman. He retired in 1932. (16)

Sir Samuel Augustus PETHEBRIDGE (1862-1918)

Born in Brisbane, Pethebridge went onto pursue a distinguished career as a public servant and military administrator culminating in a knighthood. He began with the Queensland Public Service, advancing to the Marine Board and the Queensland Naval Brigade. Pethebridge quickly gained a reputation as conscientious administrator in roles which were at times onerous. He was allocated the task of organising the reception for the arrival of the American Fleet in 1908. Initially chosen to head the force which was to occupy the German islands north of the equator he was later re-directed to replace Colonel Holmes as Administrator at Rabaul. Once again he proved conscientious and so was given considerable freedom from Australian government interference. However the task took a heavy toll on his health. He contracted malaria which permanently weakened him and forced him to return to Australia in 1917. He died in January, 1918, survived by his wife and two children. (17)

Seaforth Simpson MACKENZIE (1883-1955)

The final "pen portrait" of the men of the AN&MEF is that of the man who wrote the best-researched and most comprehensive account of the Australia's early involvement in New Guinea. Under the supervision of C.E.W. Bean, Seaforth Simpson MacKenzie wrote Volume X of the Official War history; this volume deals exclusively with the hostilities themselves as well as the following period of administration.

With previous knowledge of German and a having a legal background, MacKenzie was a good choice as assistant for Bean. However the tale behind the teller of this military story is itself, an interesting story.

In March, 1915 Mackenzie was commissioned with the rank of Major and on 3rd April he took up the position as Deputy Judge Advocate General and legal adviser to Colonel Pethebridge. He had to take on multiple roles; registrar, civil judge and supervision of District

Officers who also acted as magistrates despite the fact that they had no legal training. At times he found himself in opposition to Pethebridge and this was usually over the issue of just where their rights as an occupying force ended. From 1918 he was Acting Administrator for a time and it was in this role that he became more involved with the commercial activities of the region. From 1921 he returned to Australia where he was appointed as Principal Registrar of the High Court. He was also busily working on writing "The Australians at Rabaul" which was first published as part of Bean's history, in 1927.

About this time he purchased three over-priced commercial plantations in New Guinea. By 1932 he was heavily in debt to the Commonwealth government for money borrowed and his losses. On 28th August, 1936 he appeared in court (on the other side of the bench) on charges of forging and uttering seals of the High Court. He was convicted and sentenced to four and a half years imprisonment. His appeal was dismissed and to add to his woes his wife divorced him in 1937. Four years after his release in 1940 he re-married (to Mary Elizabeth Hanna). He died in Melbourne in 1955. (18)

Afterword

HISTORY WILL DECIDE

"History will be kind to me for I intend to write it."

(Winston Churchill)

When the decision was first made to write about Australia's campaign in New Guinea during the Great War there were certain things that I already knew and understood. I was aware that six members of Australian military and naval forces died there. I also knew that, despite the fact that this event occurred eight months before Gallipoli, comparatively speaking, little had been written about it and that many people had not heard of this campaign.

For a long time I resisted using the term, "Baptism of Fire" when discussing the event. Speakers at ANZAC Day ceremonies frequently use the terms "Baptism of Fire" and "Forging our new nation" when referring to the Gallipoli landings. However I came to change my point of view. The New Guinea campaign was the first time that Australian men were formulated into Australian units by Australians; the first time Australians were equipped by an Australian Commonwealth government and the first time Australians had entered a war begun after Federation. In that sense it was truly our "Baptism of Fire".

As early as September, 1914 there were patriotic Australians who saw this campaign as a "baptism" for the new nation.

"The recent triumph of our brave boys in securing once again to us, German New Guinea must send a thrill of joy throughout the Commonwealth… It is our first, and let us devoutly hope, our last, baptism of blood…" (1)

Of course Australia was under close British supervision, guidance, assistance and direction. The Australian government was given the task (perhaps asked); it was told not to expect future control over New Guinea if and when it succeeded. But it was still their task and they saw it through to its completion.

The hostilities were certainly not on a large scale. Nor was the acquisition of New Guinea a major prize. It did have some economic benefits but the area was not of major strategic significance as the Great War was mainly fought in the European arena. The Germans no longer had wireless stations in our region. Thanks to that fact and the fact that Australia possessed a not insignificant naval force, the German Navy did not pose as large a threat in our region as they could have done.

Compared to the horrendous losses of Gallipoli and the Western Front our losses in New Guinea were minor. But they were still significant. As discussed earlier, the men who fought there did not deserve to be derided as "Coconut Lancers". Bean's defence of them was forthright, even heated. Rightly so. Remember that Bean, a keen and intelligent observer, saw several theatres of the Great War.

So I chose to use the term "Baptism of Fire". But this was in no way an attempt to undermine the legendary status of the Gallipoli campaign. From the outset this campaign captured the imagination of the Australian public. Reports filtering back of the horrendous loss of life were widely read and discussed. By comparison newspaper accounts of the New Guinea campaign were much shorter and were not always near the front of the paper.

In the years which have passed since the Gallipoli landings its legendary status has grown. When discussed in history classes, apart from the voice of the teacher, you can hear a pin drop. Young people, many with no direct link to returned service men and women, want to learn about Gallipoli. The numbers of those who fought in our wars may be declining but the same can't be said about the numbers attending commemorative services.

Again, rightly so. Nor is their support an attempt to glorify War. It is simply a desire to better appreciate the personal sacrifices made whether they were on the battlefield or here at home. Over the years I have watched countless videos, heard numerous interviews, read large numbers of personal accounts from those who fought in our wars.

I have yet to come across one man or woman who thought their battle experiences were a part of the best time of their lives. The vast majority condemn War as senseless and wasteful. Bewilderment and sadness are the prevailing emotions expressed.

But I digress… my use of the term, "Baptism of Fire" was purely a reflection of the chronology, not the significance, of events involving Australia in World War I.

As outlined in an earlier chapter, the New Guinea campaign saw the achievements of many "firsts" for the fledgling nation. Most of these consisted of military matters. But the campaign also ushered Australia into the realm of administering and supervising a nation other than itself; a "nation in waiting".

It also led to the involvement of that fast-growing power, Japan, with island possessions just north of New Guinea. This was to have quite catastrophic consequences, not just for Australia, but also most notably, for the United States a generation later, during World War II. World War I did not just usher in the fall of European empires (Ottoman, Austrian, Russian and German). It also changed forever the strategic significance of the Pacific region as well as the balance of power in that region.

There is no doubt that the Gallipoli campaign helped to define "who we are". It was significant to the Australian psyche; it contributed much to Australia's image overseas and much to how Australians view themselves. This campaign was part of our response to the needs of Britain, a nation with which we shared a common cultural, political, legal and historical heritage.

The New Guinea campaign, on the other hand, involved Australia with an area, unlike Britain, which was located close-by but entirely different in nature to itself. The link was geographical not historical. Australia's involvement in New Guinea had more to do with its future than it had to do with its past.

The Australian campaign which successfully claimed Germany's New Guinea possessions had significance far beyond those hectic days in September, 1914. It had consequences for those who took part and also their families back home. These could have been those associated with loss and bereavement but in many cases they were pivotal events. Many of the men involved took new directions in their lives; some went on to achieve greatness.

Towards the end of the war, Prime Minister, Billy Hughes, demanded that Australia be awarded individual representation at the

Versailles Peace Conference. In this he was unsuccessful. As shown earlier, Australia did, however, gain post-war control over New Guinea under a protectorate supervised by the League of Nations. As New Guinea moved towards full independence (finally achieved in 1975) Australia's role there changed format a number of times.

The point remains that this pattern of events came about as the result of developments which took place in the second half of the nineteenth century. Germany strove to expand its colonial interests (in the latter half of the nineteenth century) just as Australian national sentiment was coming to fruition. Hence the concerns of the Queensland government, expressed in the 1880s, as outlined in an earlier chapter. This in turn led to Australia's allocation to the task of assuming control over German possessions in the Pacific region. The finale came with the heroic deeds of the men of the AN&MEF in September, 1914.

No longer should they be our oft-forgotten heroes, known only to a few.

APPENDIX: *AE1* HONOUR ROLL

Royal Navy Personnel

Name and Rank	Place of Birth	Age
BESANT, Lieutenant-Commander Thomas Fleming	England	30
MOORE, Lieutenant Charles Lewis	Ireland	26
SCARLETT, Lieutenant The Honourable Leopold Florence	England	25
BARTON, Leading Stoker Sidney Charles	England	29
DANCE, Signalman George	England	27
DENNIS, AB Seaman Frederick George	England	28
GOUGH, Stoker Henry Joseph	England	31
GUILBERT, Petty Officer Thomas Martin	England	32
GUILD, Stoker First Class James	Scotland	30
GUY, Leading Stoker William Elliott	England	34
HODGE, Petty Officer Henry	England	34
HODGKIN, Able Seaman George	England	27
LOWE, Acting Chief ERA 2 Thomas Frederick	England	38
MARSLAND, CERA2 John Albert	England	33
MEEK, Acting Leading Stoker John William	England	27
STRETCH, Chief Stoker Harry	England	37
TRIBE, Petty Officer William	England	33
WILSON, Chief ERA 2nd Class Joseph William	England	34
WOODLAND, Able Seaman Frederick William	England	32

Royal Australian Navy Personnel

Name and Rank	Place of Birth	Age
BAKER, Telegraphist Cyril Lefroy	Tasmania	21
BLAKE, Stoker First Class Ernest Fleming	Queensland	22
BRAY, Stoker First Class John James	Victoria	23
CORBOULD, Leading Seaman Gordon Clarence	NSW	26
FETTES, ERA3 James Alexander	NSW	29
FISHER, Able Seaman Arthur Henry	England	31
HOLT, Stoker First Class Richard Baines	England	34
JARMAN, Able Seaman Jack	Victoria	21
MOLONEY, Stoker Petty Officer, John Joseph	Queensland	25
MESSENGER, ERA3 John	Victoria	27
REARDON, Able Seaman John	New Zealand	23
SMALL, Petty Officer Robert	Scotland	26
THOMAS, Able Seaman James Benjamin	England	30
WADDILOVE, Stoker Petty Officer William Alfred	Victoria	29
WILSON, Stoker Percy Lawrence	England	25
WRIGHT, Stoker Petty Officer Charles Frederick	England	25

Of the sixteen men serving with the Royal Australian Navy, four were born in the United Kingdom, one was born in New Zealand.

REFERENCES

Chapter 2 The Race for Empire

1. DR. POCKLEY. (1914, September 14). *The Sydney Morning Herald* (NSW: 1842–1954), p. 8. Retrieved 30 June, 2013, from http://nla.gov.au/nla.news-article15551201.
2. Mackenzie, Seaforth S. "The Australians at Rabaul." *Official History of Australia in the War of 1914–1918*, edited by C. E .W. Bean, vol. X, 8th edition. Sydney: Angus and Robertson, 1940, p. 2.
3. Ibid., p. 4.

Chapter 3 Duty Calls

1. *Charles Bingham Elwell, Royal Navy Service Record.* Kew, UK: The National Archive, Vol. 8, Part 2, ADM 196/47/142.
2. DR. POCKLEY. (1914, September 14). *The Sydney Morning Herald* (NSW: 1842 - 1954), p. 8. Retrieved April 1, 2013, from http://nla.gov.au/nla.news-article15551201.
3. *Item 01: Brian Coldin Antill Pockley papers, 1910-1917.* With permission of the Pockley family. State Library of New South Wales, MLMSS 1092 / Item1, pp. 1-3. Retrieved April 3, 2013, from http://acms.sl.nsw.gov.au/item/itemdetailpaged.aspx?itemid=912949.
4. Mackenzie, Seaforth S. "The Australians at Rabaul." *Official History of Australia in the War of 1914–1918*, edited by C. E .W. Bean, vol. X, 8th edition. Sydney: Angus and Robertson, 1940, pp. 5-6.
5. Ibid., p. 23.
6. *The Navy in New Guinea in 1914.* Naval Historical Society of Australia. Retrieved March 10, 2013, from http://www.navyhistory.org.au/the-navy-in-new-guinea-in-1914/.
7. Mackenzie, op. cit., p. 29.
8. Ibid., p. 4.
9. Ibid., pp. 46-48.
10. Travers, B .H. "Holmes, William (1862-1917)." *Australian Dictionary of Biography*, National Centre of Biography, Australian National University. Retrieved March 19, 2013, from http://adb.anu.edu.au/biography/holmes-william-6717/text11599.
11. Mackenzie, op. cit., p. 25.
12. SECOND MAN TO ENLIST IN AIF (1938, April 12). *The Sydney Morning Herald* (NSW : 1842 - 1954), p. 16. Retrieved July 3, 2013, from http://nla.gov.au/nla.news-article17456085.
13. Mackenzie, op. cit., p. 25.

Chapter 4 The Readiness is All

NOTE: NAA – National Archives of Australia http://www.naa.gov.au/

1. NAA: Series CP979/2, Control Symbol 4894, Miller W.
2. Mackenzie, Seaforth S. "The Australians at Rabaul." *Official History of Australia in the War of 1914–1918*, edited by C. E .W. Bean, vol. X, 8th edition. Sydney: Angus and Robertson, 1940, p. 26.
3. "Eulogy: C. E. Manning" in *The Kings School Magazine*, No. 118. Sydney: The Kings School. December, 1916. Academic and attendance details of Manning brothers provided by The Kings School Archive Collection.
4. NAA: Series B2455, Manning C.E., NAA: Series B2455, Manning G.O.
5. *Item 01: Brian Coldin Antill Pockley papers, 1910-1917.* With permission of the Pockley family. State Library of New South Wales, MLMSS 1092 / Item1, transcript. Retrieved March 4, 2013, from http://acms.sl.nsw.gov.au/item/itemdetailpaged.aspx?itemid=912949.
6. ON THE BERRIMA. (1914, September 7). *The Sydney Morning Herald* (NSW: 1842 - 1954), p. 8. Retrieved March 7, 2013, from http://nla.gov.au/nla.news-article15534765

Chapter 5 Shaping Up: Training and Preparations

1. Mackenzie, Seaforth S. "The Australians at Rabaul." *Official History of Australia in the War of 1914–1918*, edited by C. E .W. Bean, vol. X, 8th edition. Sydney: Angus and Robertson, 1940, pp. 36-37.
2. Ibid., p. 46.
3. Ibid., p. 35.

Chapter 6 Into Battle

1. "Letter from Captain Brian Pockley to his family dated 10 September, 1914." *Item 01: Brian Coldin Antill Pockley papers, 1910-1917.* With permission of the Pockley family. State Library of New South Wales, MLMSS 1092 / Item1, transcript. Retrieved March 10, 2013, from http://acms.sl.nsw.gov.au/item/itemdetailpaged.aspx?itemid=912949.
2. "Letter from O.W. Gillam to C.E.W. Bean 30 March 1925." *Records of C.E.W. Bean - AWM38, 3DRL606 Folders.* Australian War Memorial, AWM38, 3DRL606/258/1 - 1914–1927, p. 20. Retrieved March 7, 2013, from https://www.awm.gov.au/collection/records/awm38/3drl606/awm38-3drl606-258-1.pdf.
3. War Office. *Field Service Pocket Book, 1914.* London: H.M. Stationery Office, 1914. Chapter 8, part 47, Section II, Paragraph 6.
4. Mackenzie, Seaforth S. "The Australians at Rabaul." *Official History of Australia in the War of 1914–1918*, edited by C. E .W. Bean, vol. X, 8th edition. Sydney: Angus and Robertson, 1940, p. 55.
5. "Letter from R.R. Garran to C.E.W. Bean, 29 October 1925." *Records of C.E.W. Bean - AWM38, 3DRL606 Folders.* Australian War Memorial, AWM38, 3DRL606/258/1 -

1914–1927, p. 17. Retrieved March 7, 2013, from https://www.awm.gov.au/collection/records/awm38/3drl606/awm38-3drl606-258-1.pdf.

6. "Letter from R. G. Bowen to C. E. W. Bean, 8 January 1926." *Records of C.E.W. Bean - AWM38, 3DRL606 Folders.* Australian War Memorial, AWM38, 3DRL606/258/1 - 1914 - 1927, p. 19. Retrieved March 7, 2013, from https://www.awm.gov.au/collection/records/awm38/3drl606/awm38-3drl606-258-1.pdf.
7. "Letter from R. G. Bowen to C. E. W. Bean, 18 August 1925." *Records of C.E.W. Bean - AWM38, 3DRL606 Folders.* Australian War Memorial, AWM38, 3DRL606/258/1 - 1914 - 1927, p. 14. Retrieved March 7, 2013, from https://www.awm.gov.au/collection/records/awm38/3drl606/awm38-3drl606-258-1.pdf.

Chapter 7 Pushing On

1. BULLET PROOF JACK TAR. (1914, October 26). *Evening News* (Sydney, NSW: 1869 - 1931), p. 6. Retrieved July 29, 2013, from http://nla.gov.au/nla.news-article114235762.
2. Ibid.
3. RABAUL. (1914, October 6). *The Sydney Morning Herald* (NSW: 1842 - 1954), p. 6. Retrieved June 20, 2013, from http://nla.gov.au/nla.news-article15536352.
4. *The London Gazette.* 28 January 1916. Supplement No. 29455. *The London Gazette.* 11 July 1916. Supplement No. 29664.

Chapter 8 The Siege of Toma

1. Mackenzie, Seaforth S. "The Australians at Rabaul." *Official History of Australia in the War of 1914–1918*, edited by C. E .W. Bean, vol. X, 8th edition. Sydney: Angus and Robertson, 1940, p. 52.
2. Ibid., p. 75.
3. Jose, Arthur W. "The Royal Australian Navy 1914–1918" in *Official History of Australia in the War of 1914–1918*, edited by C. E .W. Bean, vol. IX, 8th edition. Sydney: Angus and Robertson, 1940, p. 98.
4. Burnell, Frederick S. *How Australia Took German New Guinea: An Illustrated Record of the Australian Naval & Military Expeditionary Force.* Sydney, New South Wales: W. C. Penfold & Co, 1915, p. 19.
5. RABAUL. (1914, October 6). *The Sydney Morning Herald* (NSW: 1842 - 1954), p. 6. Retrieved June 20, 2013, from http://nla.gov.au/nla.news-article15536352.
6. Mackenzie, op. cit., p. 82.
7. Ibid., p. 83.
8. Ibid., p. 84.
9. Ibid., p. 91.
10. Ibid., p. 40.
11. Ibid., p. 73.

Chapter 9 Role of the RAN

1. *Records of C.E.W. Bean - AWM38, 3DRL606 Folders*. Australian War Memorial, AWM38, 3DRL606/264/1 - 1914 - 1938. Retrieved June 8, 2013, from https://www.awm.gov.au/collection/records/awm38/3drl606/awm383drl606-264-1.pdf.
2. Jose, Arthur W. "The Royal Australian Navy 1914–1918" in *Official History of Australia in the War of 1914–1918*, edited by C. E .W. Bean, vol. IX, 8th edition. Sydney: Angus and Robertson, 1940, p. 38.
3. Ibid., pp. 112-113.
4. Mackenzie, Seaforth S. "The Australians at Rabaul." *Official History of Australia in the War of 1914–1918*, edited by C. E .W. Bean, vol. X, 8th edition. Sydney: Angus and Robertson, 1940, pp. 115-16.
5. Jose, op. cit., pp. 120-121.
6. Ibid., pp. 121, footnote.
7. Mackenzie, op. cit., p. 89.
8. Ibid., pp. 144-146.
9. "Notes on Volume X… PAGE 125." *Records of C.E.W. Bean - AWM38, 3DRL606 Folders*. Australian War Memorial, AWM38, 3DRL606/258/1 - 1914 - 1927, p. 43. Retrieved March 2, 2013, from https://www.awm.gov.au/collection/records/awm38/3drl606/awm38-3drl606-264-1.pdf.
10. Mackenzie, op. cit., p. 117.
11. Ibid., pp. 118-120.

Chapter 10 Tragedy amidst Victory

1. Jose, Arthur W. "The Royal Australian Navy 1914–1918." *Official History of Australia in the War of 1914–1918*, edited by C. E .W. Bean, vol. IX, 8th edition. Sydney: Angus and Robertson, 1940, p. 97.
2. Seal, Dr Graham. *Finding the Lost Submarine: The Mystery of AE1*. Submarine Institute of Australia, Submarines in Australia, World War I. Retrieved March 2, 2013, from http://www.submarineinstitute.com/userfiles/File/AE1 - THE LOST SUBMARINE.pdf.
3. Sarah Whyte and Tim Barlass, "Race to solve the Mystery of the AE1." *Sun-Herald*. 29 January, 2012, p. 11.
4. OUT OF THE WOLF'S FANGS. (1918, December 18). *The Register* (Adelaide, SA: 1901 - 1929), p. 9. Retrieved July 29, 2013, from http://nla.gov.au/nla.news-article60532467.
5. Jose, op. cit., p. 132. Quote "Memo from the Naval board."
6. Chief of the General Staff, *Australia. First World War Diaries - AWM4, 1/1/2PART1 - September 1914*, p. 121. Retrieved July 29, 2013, from https://www.awm.gov.au/collection/records/awm4/1/1/awm4-1-1-2part1.pdf
7. Jose, op. cit., pp. 129-130.
8. Ibid., p. 131.
9. Ibid., pp. 136-137.

Chapter 11 Mission (partly) Accomplished

NOTE: NAA – National Archives of Australia http://www.naa.gov.au/

1. "Glimpses of New Guinea." *Records of C.E.W. Bean - AWM38, 3DRL606 Folders*. Australian War Memorial, AWM38, 3DRL606/258/1 - 1914 - 1927, p. 50. Retrieved March 7, 2013, from https://www.awm.gov.au/collection/records/awm38/3drl606/awm38-3drl606-258-1.pdf.
2. Ibid., p. 51. "Our Mandate… To the editor of the Herald."
3. *RAN Sea Power Centre - Australia*. Website: http://www.navy.gov.au/history/sea-power-centre
4. "Letter to Wing-Cmdr. Harrison, 9 March, 1934." *Records of C.E.W. Bean - AWM38, 3DRL606 Folders*. Australian War Memorial, AWM38, 3DRL606/258/1 - 1914 - 1927, p. 5. Retrieved March 7, 2013, from https://www.awm.gov.au/collection/records/awm38/3drl606/awm38-3drl606-258-1.pdf.
5. Ibid., pp. 11-12. "Reply to Bean's Inquiry."
6. Mackenzie, Seaforth S. "The Australians at Rabaul." *Official History of Australia in the War of 1914–1918*, edited by C. E .W. Bean, vol. X, 8th edition. Sydney: Angus and Robertson, 1940, p. 74.
7. Ibid., p. 73.
8. "Report on the death of Petty Officer Williams." *POPPY By Bonnie Nairn Antill Pockley*. Website: http://www.duckdigital.net/Bonnie/poppy30.html
9. Maguire Major F. A. *Item 02 : Letters to Dr. Antill Pockley regarding his sons Brian and John Pockley, and other papers, 21 August 1890 - 19 February 1926*. Sydney: State Library of New South Wales, Call Number MLMSS 1092 / Item 2. Retrieved June 14, 2013, from http://acms.sl.nsw.gov.au/item/itemDetailPaged.aspx?itemID=912961
10. *The London Gazette*, January, 1916, p. 449.
11. Ibid., p. 449.
12. WAR DAY BY DAY. (1914, October 16). *Daily Herald* (Adelaide, SA: 1910 - 1924), p. 5. Retrieved July 29, 2013, from http://nla.gov.au/nla.news-article105464817.
13. Worthington, Angus Hermon (1919). *Our island captures: being an account of the operations of the Australian Expeditionary Force in the South Pacific Ocean, 1914* [electronic resource]. Adelaide: Hassell & Son, 1919. Retrieved July 10, 2013, from http://trove.nla.gov.au/version/166191129.
14. Mackenzie, op. cit., p. 61.
15. Ibid., p. 61.
16. Johnston, Brigadier-General G. J. *Extract from District Order No. 436, Part 1*. Rabaul, 12 July 1919.
17. NAA: Series B2455, Pockley B.C.A.
18. Lincoln, Merrilyn. "Bowen, Rowland Griffiths (1879–1965)." *Australian Dictionary of Biography*, National Centre of Biography, Australian National University. Retrieved June 30, 2013, from http://adb.anu.edu.au/biography/bowen-rowland-griffiths-5311/text8925.
19. NAA: Series CP979/2, Control Symbol 2, Skillen D.S.

20. "Recruiter Timothy Sullivan." *The Advertiser* (Adelaide), 19 August, 1915, p. 6. Retrieved February 27, 2013, from http://trove.nla.gov.au/ndp/del/printArticleJpg/5478093.
21. NAA: Series B2455, Tonks J.H.

Chapter 12 German Defiance

1. Lincke, Robert. "The Influence of German Surveying on the Development of New Guinea." *XXIII FIG Congress in Munich, Germany.* 8-13 October, 2006, p. 10.
2. Ibid., p. 10.
3. Ibid., pp. 11-12.
4. AUSTRALIA AND NEW GUINEA... German Allegations of 'Slave-Hunting'. (1919, November 14). The Register (Adelaide, SA: 1901 - 1929), p. 6. Retrieved June 20, 2013, from http://nla.gov.au/nla.news-article63120400.
5. WHO IS DETZNER? (1919, November 17). *The Argus* (Melbourne, Vic: 1848 - 1957), p. 5. Retrieved June 20, 2013, from http://nla.gov.au/nla.news-article4653238.
6. WHO IS DETZNER? (1919, November 15). *The Argus* (Melbourne, Vic: 1848 - 1957), p. 21. Retrieved June 20, 2013, from http://nla.gov.au/nla.news-article4654012.

Chapter 13 German Resentment... Rough Justice

NOTE: NAA – National Archives of Australia http://www.naa.gov.au/

1. Mackenzie, Seaforth S. "The Australians at Rabaul." *Official History of Australia in the War of 1914–1918*, edited by C. E .W. Bean, vol. X, 8th edition. Sydney: Angus and Robertson, 1940, p. 125.
2. Australian Light Horse Studies Centre, Project Leader. *Flogging Germans, New Guinea, 30 November 1914 [Proclamation: Graphic].* Australian Light Horse Studies Centre, 5 January, 2010. Retrieved March 5, 2013, from http://alh-research.tripod.com/Light_Horse/index.blog?topic_id=1106539.
3. NAA: Series A2, Control Symbol 1917/3615 PART 4, Item Barcode 867740. "German New Guinea - Flogging of certain German subjects at Rabaul." p. 9.
4. Ibid., p. 10.
5. Mackenzie, op. cit., p. 262.
6. Ibid., p. 261.
7. NAA: op. cit., pp. 46-47.

Chapter 14 The Australians as Administrators

1. Mackenzie, Seaforth S. "The Australians at Rabaul." *Official History of Australia in the War of 1914–1918*, edited by C. E .W. Bean, vol. X, 8th edition. Sydney: Angus and Robertson, 1940, p. 189.
2. Ibid., p. 191.

3. RAN. HMAS *Encounter* (I). Royal Australian Navy website. Home » The Fleet » Ships, Boats & Craft, 2013. Retrieved March 22, 2013, from http://www.navy.gov.au/hmas-encounter-i.
4. NAA: Series CP979/2, Control Symbol 4894, Miller W.
5. Mackenzie, op. cit., pp. 178, 197-198.
6. "The Taking of Bougainville." Chronicle (Adelaide, SA: 1895 - 1954), January 23, 1915, p. 42. Retrieved July 15, 2013, from http://nla.gov.au/nla.news-article95772849.
7. Mackenzie, op. cit., pp. 308-309.
8. Ibid., pp. 232-233.
9. Ibid., p. 306.
10. Ibid., p. 303.

Chapter 15 Garrison Life

NOTE: NAA – National Archives of Australia http://www.naa.gov.au/

1. Mackenzie, Seaforth S. "The Australians at Rabaul." *Official History of Australia in the War of 1914–1918*, edited by C. E .W. Bean, vol. X, 8th edition. Sydney: Angus and Robertson, 1940, p. 317.
2. Ibid., pp. 195-196.
3. Meade, Kevin. *Heroes before Gallipoli*. Milton, Queensland: John Wiley & Sons Australia Ltd, 2005, pp. 95-96. Navy records. *War Diary of Australian Naval and Military Expeditionary Force*. AWM36, BUNDLE 46 - PART 1, AWM36, BUNDLE 46 - PART 2. Australian War Memorial.
4. Mackenzie, op. cit., p. 329.
5. Ibid., p. 329.
6. Davies, Margrit. *Public health and colonialism: the case of German New Guinea, 1884-1914*. Thesis (M.A.) Australian National University. Canberra: National Library of Australia, Libraries Australia ID 22485365. 1992, p. 51.
7. British Administration. "Government Gazette – German New Guinea, Vol.1, No.1, 15th October, 1915." *Records of C.E.W. Bean - AWM38, 3DRL606 Folders*. Australian War Memorial, AWM38, 3DRL606/258/1 - 1914 - 1927, p. 11. Retrieved July 10, 2013, from https://www.awm.gov.au/collection/records/awm38/3drl606/awm38-3drl606-258-1.pdf.
8. NAA: Series B2455, Read J.
9. NAA: Series B2455, Lindsay A.J.
10. NAA: Series B2455, Morgan J.
11. British Administration, op. cit., pp. 10-11.
12. Ibid., p. 8.
13. Currey, Andrew. *Close Shaves*. Canberra: Australian War Memorial, 3 March 2011, pp. 1-2. Retrieved July 7, 2013, from http://www.awm.gov.au/blog/2011/03/03/close-shaves/.
14. NAA: Series B2455, Wates A.M.
15. NAA: Series B2455, Manning G.O.

16. British Administration, op. cit., p. 10.
17. Worthington, Angus Hermon. *Our Island Captures: being an account of the operations of the Australian Expeditionary Force in the South Pacific Ocean.* Electronic resource. Adelaide: Hassell & Son, 1914, p. 53. Retrieved July 10, 2013, from http://trove.nla.gov.au/work/152481127.
18. A.N. and M.E.F. *Passed by Censor XMAS 1914-1918.* Electronic resource. Rabaul: A.N. and M.E.F., 1918. Retrieved July 10, 2013 from http://handle.slvvic.gov.au/10381/151896.
19. Mackenzie, op. cit., p. 332.
20. Ibid., p. 333.
21. Ibid., p. 331.
22. "Battalion N & M Forces programme of concert" in *Concert and Theatre Programs Collection - First World War 1914-1918.* Canberra: Australian War Memorial. ID number Series 4, Sub-series 1, File 33, Item 2.

Chapter 16 What became of…?

NOTE: NAA – National Archives of Australia http://www.naa.gov.au/

1. NAA: CP979/2, Eitel C.C.
2. NAA: Series B2455, Miller W. NAA: Series B2455, Miller W. Miller Family History records.
3. NAA: Series No. A6769, Hill G.A. AWM: Hill, Gerald Ashby (Lieutenant-Commander). ID number: 1DRL/0351. *Australian War Memorial.* Retrieved 20 July, 1913 from http://www.awm.gov.au/collection/1DRL/0351 NAVAL WEDDING. (1915, March 6). *Evening News* (Sydney, NSW : 1869 - 1931), p. 5. Retrieved July 20, 2013, from http://nla.gov.au/nla.news-article115823749
4. NAA: Series B2455, Harcus J.L.
5. NAA: Series B2455, Bond T.A. NAA: Series CP979/2, Bond T.A.
6. Argent, A. "Beardsmore, Robert Henry (1873-1959)." *Australian Dictionary of Biography*, National Centre of Biography, Australian National University. Retrieved 23 May, 2013 from http://adb.anu.edu.au/biography/beardsmore-robert-henry-5169/text8683.
7. Broun, Malcolm D. "Dovey, Wilfred Robert (Bill), (1894-1969)." *Australian Dictionary of Biography*, National Centre of Biography, Australian National University. Retrieved 20 May, 2013 from http://adb.anu.edu.au/biography/dovey-wilfred-robert-bill-10039/text17701.
8. "Maguire, Frederick Arthur (1888-1953)." (2010) In *Trove*, National Library of Australia. Retrieved 20 May, 2013 from http://nla.gov.au/nla.party-638162.
9. NAA: Series B2455, Manning C.E.
10. Mackenzie, Seaforth S. "The Australians at Rabaul." *Official History of Australia in the War of 1914–1918*, edited by C. E .W. Bean, vol. X, 8th edition. Sydney: Angus and Robertson, 1940, p. 143.
11. Ibid., p. 124.

12. Travers, B. H. "Holmes, William (1862-1917)." *Australian Dictionary of Biography*, National Centre of Biography, Australian National University. Retrieved 19 March, 2013 from http://adb.anu.edu.au/biography/holmes-william-6717/text11599.
13. Hill, A. J. "Howse, Sir Neville Reginald (1863-1930)." *Australian Dictionary of Biography*, National Centre of Biography, Australian National University. Retrieved 4 July, 2013 from http://adb.anu.edu.au/biography/howse-sir-neville-reginald-6753.
14. Lincoln, Merrilyn. "Bowen, Rowland Griffiths, (1879-1965)." *Australian Dictionary of Biography,* National Centre of Biography, Australian National University. Retrieved 30 June, 2013 from http://adb.anu.edu.au/biography/bowen-rowland-griffiths-5311/text8925.
15. Finlay, C. H. "Heritage, Francis Bede (1877-1934)." *Australian Dictionary of Biography,* National Centre of Biography, Australian National University. Retrieved 21 March, 2013 from http://adb.anu.edu.au/biography/heritage-francis-bede-6648.
16. Martin, John Stanley. "Lyng, Jens Sorensen (1868-1941)." *Australian Dictionary of Biography*, National Centre of Biography, Australian National University. Retrieved 20 May 2013 from http://adb.anu.edu.au/biography/lyng-jens-sorensen-13059/text23615.
17. Mawer, Granville Allen. "Pethebridge, Sir Samuel Augustus (1862–1918)." *Australian Dictionary of Biography*, National Centre of Biography, Australian National University, 1988. Retrieved July 27, 2013, from http://adb.anu.edu.au/biography/pethebridge-sir-samuel-augustus-8029/text13997.
18. McNicoll, Ronald. "Mackenzie, Seaforth Simpson, (1883-1955)", *Australian Dictionary of Biography*, National Centre of Biography, Australian National University. Retrieved 18 March, 2013 from http://adb.anu.edu.au/biography/Mackenzie-seaforth-simpson-7390/text12849

Afterword History will Decide

1. "AUSTRALIAN PATRIOTS Letter to the Editor." (1914, September 16). *The Argus* (Melbourne, Vic: 1848–1957), p. 9. Retrieved July 12, 2013, from http://nla.gov.au/nla.news-article10806796.

BIBLIOGRAPHY

Books

Burnell, Frederick S. *How Australia Took German New Guinea: An Illustrated Record of the Australian Naval & Military Expeditionary Force*. Sydney, New South Wales: W.C. Penfold & Co, 1915.

Grattan, Clinton H. *The Southwest Pacific to 1900*. Ann Arbor: University of Michigan Press, 1963. Mainly used as a reference for early European exploration and involvement in the New Guinea area.

Hiery, Hermann J. *The Neglected War: The German South Pacific and the Influence of World War I*. Honolulu, Hawaii: University of Hawaii Press, 1995. The focus with this book is the plight of the indigenous peoples of the Pacific region under European colonial control.

Jose, Arthur W. "The Royal Australian Navy 1914–1918" in *Official History of Australia in the War of 1914–1918*, edited by C. E .W. Bean, vol. IX, 8th edition. Sydney: Angus and Robertson, 1940.

Mackenzie, Seaforth S. "The Australians at Rabaul" in *Official History of Australia in the War of 1914–1918*, edited by C. E .W. Bean, vol. X, 8th edition. Sydney: Angus and Robertson, 1940.

Meade, Kevin. *Heroes before Gallipoli*. Milton, Queensland: John Wiley & Sons Australia Ltd, 2005.

Newspaper Articles

"On the Berrima." *Sydney Morning Herald*. 7 September, 1914.

"Brilliant Student and Athlete." *Sydney Morning Herald*. 14 September, 1914.

"Australian Patriots: Letter to the Editor." *Argus*, Melbourne. 16 September, 1914.

"Naval Wedding." *Evening News*. 6 March, 1915.

"Battle-scarred Able Seaman Sullivan." *Daily Herald*, Adelaide. 13 August, 1915.

"Bullet Proof Jack Tar." *Sydney Morning Herald*. 6 October, 1914.

"The Taking of Bougainville." *The Advertiser* (Adelaide). 18 January, 1915.

"The Taking of Bougainville." *Barrier Miner* (Broken Hill). 20 January, 1915.

"The Taking of Bougainville." *Chronicle* (Adelaide). 23 January, 1915.

"German allegations of Slave hunting." *The Register*, (Adelaide). 14 November, 1919.

"Who is Detzner?" *Argus*, (Melbourne). 15 November, 1919.

"Who is Detzner? Response." *Argus*, (Melbourne). 17 November, 1919.

"Glimpses of New Guinea." *Sydney Morning Herald*. 1 December, 1926.

"Second Man to Enlist." *Sydney Morning Herald*. 12 April, 1938.

"Alchemy of War turned Convicts into Heroes." *The Australian*. 24 April, 1990.

"Race to solve the Mystery of the AE1." *Sun Herald*. 29 January, 2012.

NOTE: Most news articles above were retrieved from Trove, the searchable online digital collection provided by the National Library of Australia, and accessible at http://trove.nla.gov.au/.

Documents

"Battalion N & M Forces programme of concert" in *Concert and Theatre Programs Collection – First World War 1914-1918*. Canberra: Australian War Memorial. ID number Series 4, Sub-series 1, File 33, Item 2.

Bean, C. E. W. *Folder, 1914 – 1927: Diaries and Notebooks*. Canberra: Australian War Memorial, ID number AWM38, 3DRL606/258/1 - 1914 – 1927.

Bean, C. E. W. *Folder, 1914 – 1938: Diaries and Notebooks*. Canberra: Australian War Memorial, ID number AWM38, 3DRL606/264/1 - 1914 – 1938.

Brian Coldin Antill Pockley papers, 1910-1917. Sydney: State Library of NSW, ID number MLMSS 1092 / Item 1.

Charles Bingham Elwell, Royal Navy Service Record. Kew, UK: The National Archive, Vol. 8, Part 2.

Davies, Margrit. *Public health and colonialism: the case of German New Guinea, 1884-1914*. Thesis (M.A.) Australian National University. Canberra: National Library of Australia, Libraries Australia ID 22485365. 1992.

"Eulogy: C. E. Manning" in *The Kings School Magazine*, No. 118. Sydney: The Kings School. December, 1916.

First Australian Imperial Force Personnel Dossiers, 1914-1920. Canberra: National Archives of Australia. ID number Series B2455.

"Formation headquarters" in *Australian Imperial Force unit war diaries, 1914-18 War*, Item No. 1/1/3 Part 1. Canberra: Australian War Memorial, ID number AWM4.

German New Guinea - Flogging of certain German subjects at Rabaul. Canberra: National Archives of Australia, ID number A2, 1917/3615 PART 4.

Government Gazette: British Administration, New Guinea. Vol. 1, No. 1. Canberra: Australian War Memorial, ID number AWM38, 3DRL606/258/1 - 1914 – 1927, 15 October, 1915.

Heritage, Keith. *Item 02: Letters to Dr Antill Pockley regarding his sons Brian and John Pockley, and other papers, 21 August 1890-19 February 1926*. Sydney: State Library of NSW, Call Number MLMSS 1092 Item 2.7 November 1914.

Kember, William. *Item 02: Letters to Dr Antill Pockley regarding his sons Brian and John Pockley, and other papers, 21 August 1890-19 February 1926*. Sydney: State Library of NSW, Call Number MLMSS 1092/Item 2.7 November 1914.

Lincke, Robert. "The Influence of German Surveying on the Development of New Guinea." *XXIII FIG Congress in Munich, Germany*. 8-13 October, 2006.

Maguire, Major F.A. *Item 02: Letters to Dr Antill Pockley regarding his sons Brian and John Pockley, and other papers,21 August 1890-19 February 1926*. Sydney: State Library of NSW, Call Number MLMSS 1092/Item 2.7 November, 1914.

Miller and Ellis Families. Papers and Records.

MILLER William - Service Number - 2775. Canberra: National Archives of Australia. ID number Series CP 979/2 Control Symbol 4894.

Official History, 1914-18 War, biographical and other research files. Canberra: Australian War Memorial, ID number AWM 43.

Rabaul Garrison AN&MEF. *Passed by Censor, Xmas 1914-1918*. Melbourne: State Library of Victoria, search ID number 940.48194 P26A.

Service cards – Navy officers. Canberra: National Archives of Australia. ID number Series A6769.

The London Gazette, 28 January, 1916.

The London Gazette, 11 July, 1916.

War Diary of the Australian Naval and Military Expeditionary Force. Canberra: Australian War Memorial, ID number AWM36 Bundle 46 Parts 1-2.

Websites

AE1 Incorporated: The search for Australia's First Submarine
http://www.ae1.org.au/

Australian Dictionary of Biography
http://adb.anu.edu.au/

Australian Light Horse Association
http://www.lighthorse.org.au/

Australian War Memorial
http://www.awm.gov.au/

National Archives of Australia
http://www.naa.gov.au/

National Library of Australia
http://www.nla.gov.au/

National Library of Australia: Trove
http://www.trove.nla.gov.au/

Naval Historical Society of Australia
http://navyhistory.org.au/

Royal Australian Navy History
http://www.navy.gov.au/history/sea-power-centre

State Library of New South Wales
http://www.sl.nsw.gov.au

Submarine Institute of Australia
http://www.submarineinstitute.com/

The Pockley Family
http://pockley.org/
http://duckdigital.net/

INDEX

Military and Naval ranks are given as at the time of hostilities in 1914. Vessels listed *(in italics)* include RAN ships involved plus others mentioned in some particular incident in the text. (E&OE).